MEDIEVAL FRESCOES

FROM THE VATICAN MUSEUMS COLLECTION

MEDIEVAL FRESCOES

FROM THE VATICAN MUSEUMS COLLECTION

An Exhibit at the Museum of Texas Tech University

Lubbock, Texas

June 2 to September 15, 2002

Medieval Frescoes from the Vatican Museums Collection
Copyright ©2002 by the Museum of Texas Tech University

Published by the Museum of Texas Tech University
Box 43191, Lubbock, Texas 79409 USA

Project Coordinator: Gary Edson
Editor at the Vatican Museums: Francesco Buranelli
Editor at Texas Tech University: Margaret Lutherer
Designer: Bonnie Bishop Design, Santa Fe, New Mexico
Production: Bonnie Bishop Design
Copyeditor: Julie Kandyba, Copygraphics, Santa Fe, New Mexico
Printer: Woods Lithographics, Phoenix, Arizona
Photographs of Vatican art work and frescoes are from the Vatican Museums
Other photographs are provided by services noted in the caption.
All photographs remain the copyright of the contributing agency.
Translation of Italian text: Stefano D'Amico and Aliza S. Wong
Translation of German text: Meredith McClain and David Luke
Translation Assistant at the Vatican Museums: Karin Jansen

ISBN: 1-929330-02-2

Front Cover: *St Catherine Asks God for Enlightenment Before the Disputation with
the Lawyers*, detached fresco, Vatican Museums.
Back Cover: *The Dead Bodies of the Converted and Burned Lawyers are Collected by
the Christians and Buried*, detached fresco, Vatican Museums.

CONTENTS

MESSAGE OF WELCOME

It is my great pleasure to welcome our many guests to one of the most significant events ever held on our campus, *Medieval Frescoes from the Vatican Museums Collection*. This exclusive event held at the Museum of Texas Tech University from June 2 through September 15, 2002 is a wonderful opportunity to showcase our beautiful campus, our outstanding museum, and the commitment to the fine arts that exists as a central mission of Texas Tech University. We are honored and humbled to have the opportunity to exhibit these priceless medieval treasures on our campus.

To the countless community volunteers who have worked for several years to make this exhibit a reality and to Gary Edson, Executive Director of the Museum of Texas Tech University and his fine staff, I offer my most sincere congratulations for an outstanding effort. To the Reverend Malcolm Neyland and the directors of the Vatican Exhibit 2002 Foundation, who first conceived of bringing a Vatican exhibit to West Texas, I offer my thanks for a wonderful vision. The reality of that vision will bring a new level of artistic appreciation to thousands of West Texas residents and to hundreds of others from around the world. Above all, the Texas Tech University community is proud to have had the honor of working with the Vatican Museums in putting together this once-in-a-lifetime exhibit of medieval frescoes.

To Dr. David Smith, Chancellor of the Texas Tech University System, and Dr. Donald Haragan, President Emeritus of Texas Tech University, I extend my sincere appreciation for your diligence in making this exhibit a reality.

We expect many visitors from around the world to enjoy these priceless treasures from the Vatican Museums Collection this summer and many more to find inspiration and valuable knowledge in the pages of this beautiful catalog. To all who visit the exhibit in person or through these pages, I offer you a most sincere welcome from the faculty, administration and students of Texas Tech University.

David J. Schmidly, Ph.D.,
President, Texas Tech University

MESSAGE OF WELCOME

It is with great joy that we greet all visitors to this historic exhibition, *Medieval Frescoes from the Vatican Museums Collection*. Throughout the ages, artistic images have contributed to the evangelization of the world. The Catholic Church has, therefore, always been a principal patron of the arts, supporting all that is noble and true, good and beautiful. Welcome.

With their focus on the zeal for holiness and love for all people manifest in the lives of Prophets and Saints, these particular objects of art reflect vital mysteries of our Christian faith. The frescoes provide viewers with a glance at our "ancestors" in the faith. By reflecting on these treasures, we can see anew what is revealed about God's plan in the Old Testament and we can renew our courage to follow the Way of Jesus Christ that is revealed in the New Testament.

The Catholic faithful of the Roman Catholic Diocese of Lubbock—and I, as bishop of this local church—are deeply indebted to the Holy Father, Pope John Paul II, for graciously granting his permission for the Vatican Museums to loan these works of art to the Church in West Texas. The generosity demonstrated by His Holiness provides the Diocese of Lubbock—in collaboration with the skilled and artful staff at Texas Tech Museum—with a dramatic opportunity to share these magnificent medieval frescoes with many who could not otherwise have seen them firsthand.

We pray that all who visit these masterpieces will realize the fullness of the message expressed in them—emotionally, intellectually, and, most important of all, spiritually. May the examples of the Prophets and Saints portrayed in these frescoes inspire us to dedicate ourselves to the mission they fulfilled so well; embracing all creation and loving all people with the spirit and love of Jesus Christ.

May the God of hope fill you with all joy and peace as you trust in him, so that you may overflow with hope by the power of the Holy Spirit. —Romans 15:13

Sincerely in His service,
Most Rev. Plácido Rodríguez, CMF
Bishop of Lubbock

MESSAGE OF APPRECIATION

This exhibit brings some of the finest art in the world to the State of Texas to foster an appreciation for art, culture, and history. The impact of great works of art is incalculable, and each fresco is a prism through which one can glimpse something of the faith, politics, and creativity of the era that witnessed its creation.

The Vatican Exhibit 2002 Foundation is proud to assist in bringing this exhibit to Lubbock and the State of Texas. Pope John Paul II, who gave his all-important permission, made the loan of these frescoes possible. His Eminence Cardinal Casaroli also generously supported the idea. We thank Archbishop Patrick Flores, DD, Metropolitan for Texas, and Bishop Placido Rodriguez, CMF, Bishop of Lubbock, for their intervention on our behalf.

The Vatican Exhibit 2002 Foundation thanks the Director of the Vatican Museums, Dr. Francesco Buranelli, and Edmund Casimir Cardinal Szoka, President of the Governatorato, Vatican City, who helped us choose these representative works. We are also sincerely grateful to Angelo Cardinal Sodano, Secretary of State, Vatican City; Mons. Gabriel Montalvo, Papal Pro-nuncio to the USA; Fr. Allen Duston, OP, Director for Patrons of the Arts in the Vatican Museums; and Fr. Richard Bourgeois, OSB, Representative for the Americas, Patrons of the Arts in the Vatican Museums.

The Vatican Exhibit 2002 Foundation acknowledges U. S. Congressman Larry Combest and U.S. Senator Kay Bailey Hutchison; Texas Governor Rick Perry; Speaker of the Texas House Pete Laney; Lieutenant Governor Bill Ratliff; Secretary of State Henry Cuellar; as well as State Senator Robert Duncan and State Representatives Bob Hunter, Carl Isett, and Tommy Merritt. We also thank Msgr. Eugene V. Clark and the New York Chapter of Patrons of the Arts in the Vatican Museums for supporting the restoration of the frescoes that were taken from Sant' Agnese fuori le Mura.

Sincerely in His Service,
Rev. Malcolm L. Neyland, M.C.L., J.C.L.
President and Executive Director, Vatican Exhibit 2002 Foundation

FOREWORD

This extraordinary exhibition of medieval frescoes offers people access to important works of art that are seldom viewed outside the Vatican Museums. As individual pieces, each detached fresco represents the essence of the creative process and the genius of artistic expression. As an exhibition, the 31 pieces present a unified view of a unique art form produced in an exceptional and often overlooked time in the history of cultural expression. The frescoes tell a powerful story of passion and devotion that is narrative and iconic.

Art has been a significant aspect of the human experience for centuries. Cultures throughout history have produced art, demonstrating that the impulse to create, to realize form and structure out of matter, and to recognize order in the world, are universal characteristics.[1]

> "Every artist when he lifts his chisel, brush, or pen, acts in accordance with patterns of thought evolved in past times. The artist's personality is formed by what he inherits from the past and his adjustment to his present; hence, the record of art is the story of men interpreting their world."[2]

The frescoes in this exhibition make evident that works of art can convey meaning in several ways. Generally, paintings portraying people or objects have one meaning, the primary level of literal representation. However, the artist may include an abstract concept that adds a secondary meaning. Because that meaning could not be explained in words, it is represented in visual shorthand drawing upon practices and standards that the viewers will recognize. For instance, in traditional Christian art, a broken wheel placed beside the figure of a woman informs the viewer that the figure represents Saint Catherine.[3] The wheel is associated with the human figure to give that image a recognized identity. Other examples of the artistic formulaic reference are the Holy Spirit symbolized by a dove and Christ by a fish. The early Christians had to be cautious in the face of religious persecution; therefore, they were predisposed to using simple and easily recognized images.[4]

In addition, a work of art often has two distinct manifestations. It is a present experience as well as a record of the past, and it may be valued and preserved for both elements. A creative aspect can be viewed as depicting a personal or social ideal presented in ways that are understandable and, therefore, accessible to being perceived by the senses. This perspective of art extends to the notion of presenting imagery that is allied directly to the emotions of the viewer. This approach complements narrative art, which uses pictures to recount events of a popular, or as with the frescoes, of a religious nature.[5]

There is no effective way to measure the influence of "artistic expression" on a particular population at any given time in the history of humankind. Scholars and conjecturers have drawn parallels between societal development and the evolving and sometimes controversial art forms that are representative of a particular time and location. The creation of images, whether sacred or secular, is inevitably influenced by the attitudes of the environment in which they are produced, as well as the talent of the artist and the materials used in the creative process.

Art has been made for many reasons—religious devotion, commemoration of people and events, adornment of utilitarian objects, and personal expression.[6] The stimulant that is a point of departure for the artist in creating an image does not have to be literal; it may be something of imagination or inspiration. The imagery or composition of the work of art such as the frescoes from St. Agnese frequently had greater symbolic meaning than pictorial significance. Dramatic and representative values are often subordinate to symbolic and mnemonic purpose. One measure of a work of art, regardless of the reasoning, is the ability of the viewer to participate in the experience that the artist has interpreted.

Painting had a strong popular appeal in the late Medieval period as an illumination of religious teaching.[7] The repertoire of symbolic subjects included scenes reflecting the annual cycle of the principal personalities, festivals, and events associated with the Church. These representations often borrowed imagery and concepts from the emperor's court at Constantinople. Christ in this genre (a style of painting that depicted scenes from everyday life) was not portrayed as a youthful shepherd, but as an enthroned deity with a dignified beard, and the Virgin Mary appeared crowned and robed like the empress as was appropriate in the courts of Eastern monarchs.[8] The artists worked with color, line, and other visual elements to communicate the stories pertinent to the time and location.

The frescoes in this exhibition illustrate the narrative role characteristic of artistic expression during the 12th through 14th centuries. The imagery combined traditions of the past with "new" ideals and meanings—they are simplified and spiritualized. The frescoes include animals, birds, and fish borrowed from Classical art to convey Christian significance. For instance the peacock, originally meaning wisdom, became the symbol for eternal life.[9] Paintings, sculptures, and frescoes also served as pictorial narratives for the illiterate. They told the stories of religious doctrine. The works of art such as the frescoes in this exhibition are ideas expressed in visual terms instead of words.

The Museum of Texas Tech University is extremely pleased and proud to host this exhibition of medieval frescoes from the Vatican Museums collection. An exhibition of this complexity requires the effort of many people including the Museum staff, Museum Association, volunteers, and community and university leaders. To identify every person contributing to the exhibition would require an inordinate amount of space, and to list a few individuals would not give credit to the multitude of workers and supporters that are the mainstay of the Museum. The exhibition is itself a celebration of community effort and pride, and it is to the community that thanks is given.

Gary Edson
Executive Director, Museum of Texas Tech University

ENDNOTES
[1] Roger Baldwin and Mark Roskill, "Art," *Grolier New Multimedia Encyclopedia.*™ 1994.
[2] David Robb and J.J. Garrison, *Art in the Western World* (revised edition), New York: Harper & Brothers Publishers. 1942.
[3] James Hall, "Iconography," *Grolier New Multimedia Encyclopedia.*™ 1994.
[4] Stella Russell, *Art in the World*, New York: Holt, Rinehart and Winston. 1984
[5] Ibid.
[6] Baldwin and Roskill, "Art."
[7] Horst de la Croix and Richard Tansey, *Gardner's Art Through the Ages* (sixth edition) New York: Harcourt Brace Jovanovich, Inc. 1975
[8] Robb and Garrison, *Art in the Western World*.
[9] Russell, *Art in the World*.

PREFACE

In proposing this exhibit to the city of Lubbock, Texas, the Vatican Museums wish to present visitors the evident results of a particularly important moment of the Museums' current history, and to offer, through these extraordinary cycles of medieval frescoes, a key to understanding both the nature and the origins of the renowned artistic collections of the Holy See.

Therefore, this is not only an exhibit in the tradition of those that, for many years, have tied the Vatican Museums to great American cultural institutions, but something more important and enthralling that will forever tie this complex operation and the City of Lubbock to the age-long history of the collections of the Roman Pontiffs. The restoration of the surviving frescoes of two important Roman medieval churches, Sant'Agnese fuori le Mura and San Nicola in Carcere, required highly skilled craftmanship and proved to be of major importance for the recovery of works that until then had been considered secondary and minor compared to Renaissance and Baroque masterpieces.

Today they have been reevaluated as precious and rare works. These particular frescoes are indeed fundamental elements in the portrayal of a broader history of the arts not only as written by the great geniuses, but also widespread in different forms and places that represent the extent of the very fabric of our civilization.

Thanks to the generosity of the people of Lubbock, these fragments have been taken from the storehouses of the Museums with renewed care and attention to be studied and recomposed, whenever possible, within the context of a complex work of restoration and recovery that is presented here, for the first time, as a whole.

The visitors of this exhibit, therefore, will be able not only to enjoy the restored beauty of the figures of saints and prophets, animals and refined ornamental motifs, but at the same time to participate in the enrichment of our collections in these great recovered treasures. This might be a first step towards new "discoveries" that could follow in a general project of re-examination and re-evaluation of all the works conserved in our Museums.

Historically, the vision of the Middle Ages as a period of obscure involution—

compared to the era of classical antiquity—to later be overcome by the Renaissance, is now outdated. Today, it is universally agreed that the centuries of the Middle Ages should be considered as a period of spiritual and artistic ferment, a period in which the necessary introspection after the fall of the established order of the Roman Empire generated a new vision of the world, fundamental in creating not only a new political order, but also new expressive means and new iconography. The intellectuals and artists of this period were even able to conceive new forms of government and new artistic canons that emphasized the rituals and sacred images of the Christian religion. By translating classical legacy into a new sensibility, they created that new current political, cultural and artistic language that still represents the common legacy of the western world.

The fragments of frescoes presented in Lubbock, rescued centuries ago from irremediable loss and dispersion, collected and preserved, have allowed us, on the one hand, to open a window onto the extraordinary period of the Roman Middle Ages, and on the other hand, to symbolically broaden our appreciation of the true nature of the artistic collections of the Vatican.

For centuries, the popes have been collecting not only precious decorative objects but also artifacts—often very fragmentary—of the great ancient Roman civilization together with those of early Christian art. The result is a collection of gathered statues and paintings—whether fragments casually found like the famous Torso of Belvedere, or artifacts expressly searched and then excavated. With the same spirit of conservation, the pontiffs have forbidden with equal determination the destruction and the dispersion of pagan works and monuments.

The exceptional Vatican collection, together with other museum collections in Rome ascribable to the initiative of the popes, has therefore become, with time, a repository of various masterpieces from many eras representing artistic forms. It has continued to expand even more recently if one considers the extensive patrimony of the Ethnology Museum or the Collection of Modern Art also including objects from civilizations and religions very different from one another but nevertheless united by the common and universal thread of beauty.

The Lubbock exhibit, along with others promoted by the Vatican Museums in many other countries around the world, also expresses the desire of the Holy See to have many people know and recognize more closely this universal heritage as part of that unselfish spirit of fruitful and peaceful spiritual exchange that has characterized the apostolic journeys of the Supreme Pontiff, John Paul II, for many years. The Vatican Museums have come closer, therefore, to human and geographic realities only apparently distant, and have written, in this way, a new chapter of their centuries old history, caring for the signs of the times and the cultural and spiritual growth of the human community.

In conclusion, we desire to point out again how, in the fragments of bright colors and images loaded with meaning, the Vatican Museums have desired to present, in this exhibit, works that have finally been recognized for their very real and extraordinary importance. The visitors from Lubbock, and those that will travel to the exhibit from the other nearby cities and states, must recognize the privilege they hold in being the first witnesses of such a historical artistic recovery, and at the same time, are strongly encouraged and warmly invited to one day follow these paintings back to Rome, to behold at least part of this exhibit—as we hope—in its permanent display in the Vatican Painting Gallery.

All this has been possible, thanks to the benevolent support of the Secretariat of State and of the Governorship of Vatican City, and to the competence of the many people operating in the civic and cultural institutions of Lubbock. I wish, in particular, to thank Rev. Father Malcolm L. Neyland who, with his extraordinary organizational skills, has created the right premises to bring this exhibit to Lubbock.

Recognition must also be given for the exceptional and efficient organization of the city authorities of Lubbock and to the whole administrative staff of Texas Tech University. I am pleased to thank in particular Dr. David Smith, Chancellor, Texas Tech University System; Dr. David Schmidly, President, Texas Tech University; Dr. John Burns, Provost, Texas Tech University; Dr. Donald Haragan, President Emeritus, Texas Tech University; Gary Edson, Executive Director, Museum of Texas Tech University; Ms. Linda Mires, Executive Administrator, Museum of Texas Tech University Association, and all those who in various ways have given their contribution to the success of this enterprise.

Francesco Buranelli
Director General of Pontifical Monuments, Museums, and Galleries

ACKNOWLEDGEMENTS

VATICAN MUSEUMS

Francesco Buranelli
Director General

Edith Cicerchia
Secretary General

Francesco Riccardi
Administrator

Byzantine, Medieval and Modern Art Department
Arnold Nesselrath
Anna Maria De Strobel

Exhibition Office
Andrea Carignani
Isabella Cordero di Montezemolo
Marta Monopoli
Diego Ortuso

Catalog Authors
Francesco Buranelli
Maurizio De Luca
Anna Maria De Strobel
Patrizio Di Nezio
Arnold Nesselrath
Serena Romano
Paola Rossi

Photographic Archives
Guido Cornini
Rosanna Di Pinto
Filippo Petrignani
Daniela Valci
Mario Vitaletti

Photographers
Felice Bono
Alessandro Bracchetti
Luigi Giordano
Danilo Pivato
Pietro Zigrossi

Restoration Laboratories
Maurizio De Luca
Massimo Alesl
Laura Baldelli
Francesca Cantisani
Eugenio Ercadi
Marco Innocenzi
Filippo Leopardi
Bruno Marocchini
Marcello Mattarocci
Bruno Mattei
Fabio Piacentini
Francesco Prantera
Marco Pratelli
Maria L. Pustka
Simone Virdia
Alessandra Zarella
Stefania Zucconi

Scientific Research Laboratory
Ulderico Santamaria
Giulia Artizzu
Maurizio Delle Rose
Fabio Morresi

Packing of the Frescoes
Montenovi Imballaggi

LUBBOCK, TEXAS

Vatican Exhibition 2002 Foundation
Malcolm Neyland
Giles McCrary
David Hentges
Donald May
Rita Schumacher

Vatican Exhibit Steering Committee
Donald Haragan
Malcolm Neyland
Gary Edson
Don Graf
Kae Hentges
Pat Jordan
Alicia Knight
Giles McCrary
Rose Mediano
Linda Mires
T.J. Patterson
Sally Post
David Seim
Gwen Stafford
Fred A. Underwood
Dave Walker
Martha York
Bishop Plácido Rodríquez, C.M.F.
ex officio

Primary Supporters and Contributors
Continental Airlines for transportation
of the frescoes
Lubbock Avalanche-Journal

City of Lubbock
Covenant Health System
Diamond M Foundation
Ershel Franklin Charitable Trust
Lubbock Visitors and Conventions
Bureau
Market Lubbock Inc.
Meadows Foundation
Texas Tech Chancellor's Council
The CH Foundation, Inc.
Trini Mendenhall Foundation
University Medical Center

*Special thanks to all the people
who helped to make this exhibition
possible.*

INTRODUCTION

FRAGMENTS OF THE ROMAN MIDDLE AGES

The extensive urbanistic history of a lively capital city such as that of the constantly evolving Rome—discussed in this catalogue within the essay authored by Paola Rossi—can explain the reason why so many monuments of its past, not only those from the archaeological age but also those of the medieval, have become irremediably lost through the centuries. The city, from its prehistory to present times, has grown upon itself, from time to time demolishing, adding, and modifying the remnants of previous periods. In particular, the rebuilding of churches and palaces, the restructuring of entire streets and neighborhoods undertaken after the unification of Italy between 1870 and the first half of the twentieth century, and the choice of Rome as the capital city of the burgeoning Italian state, have almost completely destroyed the historic ancient features that used to characterize the city. Besides the rare instances of certain famous monuments, like some splendid churches which were left intact albeit deprived of their original context, the main loss was, above all, the "minor" urban fabric of the city: the intricate alleys, the small squares, the chapels, and the less important churches of some neighborhoods of the old center. Two examples of this demolition are particularly meaningful – the neighborhood built between the Middle Ages and the Renaissance on the ruins of the Forum, destroyed in the 1930s in order to connect Piazza Venezia to the Colosseum, and the so-called "Spina dei Borghi" located between Piazza San Pietro and Castel Sant'Angelo, sacrificed in order to create room for the Via della Conciliazione, completed in 1950.

The almost exclusive attention scholars have reserved for the greatest monuments and artists of more recent times has hidden the many traces that still remain of periods less known in their complexity, such as the Roman Middle Ages. Only in the last few decades have the restorations of some medieval pictorial cycles, such as the surviving frescos of the basilica of San Paolo Fuori le Mura (with the famous portraits of the Popes) which burned in 1823, the chapel of San Lorenzo alla Scala Santa, the oratory of San Silvestro ai Santi Quattro Coronati, as well as some of the fragments remaining in the church of Santa Maria in Aracoeli, been initiated.

A great exhibit held in Castel Sant'Angelo in 1989-90 drew the attention of scholars to the entire series of "Fragmenta picta," fragments of "detached frescoes and mosaics of the Roman Middle Ages," often little known, kept in the storehouses of the greater museums of the city. It was on that occasion that some of the fragments exhibited in Lubbock today were drawn out of the storehouses of the Pinacoteca Vaticana and studied after a preliminary survey and a more structured restoration.

The "rediscovery" of two extraordinary pictorial cycles, unique in their kind, came to fill an important gap in a broader art history made up not only by the great masterpieces. From that first intervention, it became clear that the global recovery of such artistic documents, including the twenty-nine fragments from the basilica of Sant'Agnese fuori le Mura and the twenty-four from the "urban" church of San Nicola in Carcere, was not only important but necessary. The most precious fruits of the work undertaken by our museums, these most beautifully restored fragments, are now presented together for the first time.

The story of these frescoes and their removal from the original site is itself captivating and deserves to be recounted here briefly, as a context for the essays following in this catalogue. It takes us back in different ways to a period before the Middle Ages, to the rich first centuries of Christianity that represent the roots from which medieval art and culture would take their vital nourishment. The basilica of Sant'Agnese on Via Nomentana is actually one of the main early Christian sites in Rome, heir to the great cemeterial basilica near the tomb of the martyr Agnes that was constructed in 342 according to the desires of Constantina, daughter of the emperor Constantine, during a climate of peace with the Christian religion established by her father after the age of persecution. Next to the basilica, Constantina wanted to erect her own sumptuous funerary mausoleum (known today as the church of Santa Costanza), from which was taken the monumental porphyry sarcophagus that has been displayed in the Greek cross room of the Museo Pio-Clementino since 1790.

Pope Honorius I (625-638) wanted a new basilica *ad corpus* (constructed upon the tomb of the saint, and which called for the excavation of the galleries of the surrounding catacombs in order that the altar might coincide with the burial niche of the ancient grave) built next to the older one. The new church, like others in Rome, was therefore erected with the walls half underground and half projecting above ground, with the apse turned toward the great consular artery of Via Nomentana. An entrance at street level from the apse was created in order to remedy such a drop. Through it, one could access a double gallery open from the top over the main nave (improperly defined as the women's gallery) in order to be able to observe the tomb and stop next to it in prayer. It becomes apparent then the reason behind the importance and the attention this space of the galleries received throughout the centuries, and why their walls, between 1320 and 1330, were covered with precious frescoes whose themes—stories of Saint Benedict and Saint Catherine of Alexandria—were dictated by the Benedictine nuns who had inherited the complex of buildings connected to the church. However, the paintings were linked to the fortunate strategic function of their host environment and followed its destiny when, at the beginning of the seventeenth century, their importance decreased due to the decision to widen the front of the basilica's facade to allow a more comfortable access to the lower level of the naves, thus rendering useless the ancient "women's galleries."

In 1620, the frescoes, probably ruined by time, were covered with plaster and forgotten. Their rediscovery was related to the directive of blessed Pope Pius IX to care for the city's early Christian historical legacy and to a shocking episode in which he was the protagonist. On April 12, 1855, the floors of the rooms of the Sant'Agnese complex, where Pope Pius IX, other prelates, and scholars were standing, suddenly collapsed. Miraculously, nobody was injured. The pope then promoted the restoration (often with inappropriate stylistic interventions) of the whole religious complex, including the basilica, that soon revealed the hidden paintings. Detached from the walls in fragments, the frescoes were first sent to the Museo Pio Cristiano Lateranense (which exhibits many works from early Christian sites). Later, in 1925, they were definitively transferred to the storehouses of the Pinacoteca in the Vatican.

The paintings represent an important sample of studio painting, often of a very high level, although not of the quality of the works of great artists such as Cavallini, Torriti, and Giotto. However, they were largely inspired by the "modern" examples as well as by the treasure of older pictorial traditions, including that of the Eastern Byzantinian style, still thriving in medieval Rome. The cycles of the two saints, however, show the work of different hands. As the following essay by Arnold Nesselrath points out, some convincing hypotheses as to the creatorship of these works have been raised. The lives of Benedict and Catherine, portrayed with other figures and scenes of autonomous subjects, are modeled on the rich medieval hagiographic tradition, and in particular on the *Legenda Aurea* (mid 13th century), an inexhaustible source on the lives of saints, episodes, and iconography collected by Jacopo da Varagine. In the exhibit, one can recognize the scene of the inspiration of Saint Catherine in front of Emperor Massenzio (inv. 40470) when the young girl "began to dispute the incarnation of Christ in a scholarly fashion and the emperor did not know how to respond." Immediately afterwards, the wise men who had arrived in order to confute her were converted by Saint Catherine, and became "[destined]… to the attainment of the glorious palm of martyrdom (*Legenda Aurea*, life CLXVIII, of Saint Catherine)." One can well identify the different inspirational sources of pictorial style in these scenes. As well, in the scene of the beheading of the saint (inv. 40480), depicting the moment in which, while praying, "she raised her eyes to heaven" and, after hearing the voice of God, "she was beheaded and milk, instead of blood, spouted from her body" (*ibidem*), one can note the tension, so well-made, of the soldier drawing his sword. Among the scenes of Saint Benedict, one should give particular notice to the splendid fragment with the scene of the monk and the dragon (inv. 40469). This scene is remembered with ingenuous tones in Jacopo's *Legenda*: "A monk who did not want to stay in the convent any more insisted so much with Saint Benedict that he got angry and finally allowed him to go: right after the friar left the monastery he found a dragon with its mouth wide open that wanted to devour him;" his brothers arrived and, not being able to see the dragon, "they took their frightened and panting fellow back to the convent; there he promised that he would not leave any more" (*ibidem*, life XLVIII, of Saint Benedict). Another important scene, not related to the cycles of the two saints, is that which can probably be recomposed drawing up the two fragments (inv. 40519 and 40494), and which likely represents the marriage of the Virgin.

Also, the style of the frescoes of the church of San Nicola in Carcere, located on the slopes of Monte Capitolino near the Theatre of Marcello, erected by transforming three pagan temples of the ancient "Foro Olitorio" (for more information on the history of the church see the essay by Anna Maria De Strobel) reminds us of the context of the first Christian centuries, to which the church of the martyr Agnes has led us. And this despite the fact that the building cannot be dated before the High Middle Ages, and the frescoes adorning it were almost certainly realized in the occasion of an important restoration of the church in 1128. However, visitors to the exhibit who have had the opportunity to see other examples of early Christian art or to visit and study the Roman catacombs will find within the late paintings of San Nicola something of that older atmosphere. In the figures of the saints, the viewer is reminded of the sixth and seventh centuries by themes common in the art of the first Christians (such as the Baptism of Christ), by the rapid and effective ornamentation with animal and vegetal figures set in lively two-color linear frames used to decorate many underground cemeteries.

The frescoes of San Nicola in Carcere are actually a rare example of that very particular revival of early Christian figurative arts that took place in Rome in the first half of the twelfth century, and of which we have few examples. Among these we can mention part of the frescoes of the church of Santa Maria in Cosmedin (not far from San Nicola) or also, the famous mosaic that adorns the apse of the upper basilica of San Clemente.

Those frescoes looked so similar to the art of the catacombs in the eyes of their discoverer, the great Spanish archaeologist Alonso Chacón (latinized as Ciacconius)—who descended into the crypt of the church in 1591 by order of Cardinal Federico Borromeo, the church's titular—that he thought he had penetrated some cemeterial galleries of the first Christian centuries. According to his descriptions and to those of later visitors, the frescoes, of which only these traces remain, were set out to adorn the vaults and the walls of three small spaces (obtained from the old structures of the temples), directly inspired by the sepulchral niches of the catacombs. Restored by the great Milanese cardinal, the frescoes soon fell into bad conditions, until, in the middle of the nineteenth century, the crypt was heavily restored by the will of Pius IX, who ordered the detachment of the few better preserved fragments, all of which came from the first space. These fragments were transferred—as had been the previous ones—to the Museo Pio Cristiano, as works of "the early times of Christian painting" (according to the report of the director of the restoration, Gaspare Servi). In 1926, they arrived in the storehouses of the Pinacoteca Vaticana.

The iconographic program of the space that the nineteenth century project would have liked to recompose by rebuilding the structure of the original niche in the museums, appears almost complete. At the top of the vault was the scene of the Baptism that is very similar to the known examples of the fifth century that one can find in the baptisteries of Ravenna and that resembles those of the Roman catacombs that were hidden and forgotten in the Middle Ages. Around it were the four *tondos* (three of which are in the exhibit) portraying Moses and three prophets. The prophets hold scrolls with excerpts from their books or, in the case of Moses, from the *Deuteronomy* traditionally attributed to him. Different interpretations of the scrolls have been offered. They are all probably connected to the scene of the baptism of the Lord, one of the episodes in the Gospel in which Jesus shows himself as the redeeming Messiah. In this way, the text of the *Deuteronomy* ("The Lord your God will raise up for you a prophet like me from among your own brothers. You must listen to him" *Deuteronomy* 18,15) reveals the typologic relationship, dear to early Christian thought, between Moses and Christ and almost represents a quotation of the passages of the Gospel on Baptism and Transfiguration, both related to his divine manifestation ("This is my Son whom I love [...] Listen to him!" *Matthew* 17, 5; see also 3, 17 and other parallel passages). The text of *Jeremiah* 11,19 ("Like a gentle lamb led to the slaughter") is instead prophetic of the sentence pronounced by John the Baptist: "Look, the Lamb of God," Christ, "who takes away the sin of the world!" (*John* 1, 29) with his own sacrifice. The prophecy of Amos ("The Lord, the God of hosts is his name" *Amos* 4, 13) is inspired instead to Christ coming out of the waters and, as the true "Lord of hosts," from the obscurity of death, a symbolic representation of the role of baptism. However, it is the text held by the prophet Haggai ("In this place I will grant peace, declares the Lord Almighty" 2, 9), that refers to the salvation offered by God to those who join the Church, the community of the redeemed—that makes one believe more strongly that the references to the Baptism of the Lord are, in reality, also references to the baptism of the ones who believe in Him, in whom the slavery of sin and death has been defeated ("If we died with him, we will also live with him" 2 *Timothy* 2, 11).

We intend to advance the hypothesis that this underground space, unfortunately never clearly described before its destruction, could have served a baptismal function. At the center—under the "specular" painting of the immersion into the Jordan River and the dove of the Spirit, which descends on the Baptized to complete his transformation in *alter Christus*—could have been a baptismal font, probably fed by an underground source or water-bearing stratum,

discovered at the time of the restoration of the old buildings, and that followed a use already known to the early Christians. In the same way, the zoomorphic and phytomorphic decorations on the walls, as in the catacombs, would allude to salvation and life flourishing again in Christ—in the catacombs in the belief or hope beyond death, and on these walls, in the anticipated Easter joy of the believers, born again to a new life through the baptism. Finally, it is worth noting that to the bevy of animals of the early Christian repertoire were added some other animals of the medieval bestiary. These animals were added in an innovative and free updating of the older forms—among them, the heron (heir of the more ancient phoenix and a symbol of resurrection), the hare (an animal with many meanings, most often related to penance) and even the basiliscus, a fantastic animal with the body of a snake, legs, stylized wings, and sometimes the head of a rooster which served as the "lord of snakes" and an image of the "greatest enemy" (*Cecco d'Ascoli, L'Acerba*, XXX, 1, 10). Depicted in the exhibition, the basiliscus is defeated and made harmless, tamed, as had already been portrayed on the Romanesque portals, in order to demonstrate the victory of Christ over the old snake, renewed in every new baptism.

These priceless masterpieces have been restored to their original splendor due to the serious restoration completed by the deservedly renowned Laboratory for the Restoration of Paintings of our Museums under the direction of Maestro Maurizio De Luca (whose story is included in this catalog) and to the generous support of the Patrons of the Arts in the Vatican Museums and the cultural institutions of Lubbock. Today, they are displayed in Lubbock for the enlightened engagement of the local community.

Francesco Buranelli
Director General of the Pontifical Monuments, Museums, and Galleries

The history of the Vatican Museums is rooted in that unique moment of cultural fervor that was the Italian Renaissance. Many popes and men of the curia of the fifteenth and sixteenth centuries were learned humanists and passionate interpreters of the rediscovery of the literary and artistic legacy of antiquity of which Rome still had grandiose monumental remains. The rise to the papal throne of these men, who were tied to the more lively intellectual circles, or to the families—often of Florentine origins—who were engaged in the collecting of ancient documents and works of art, led the Papal institution, after the already enlightened centuries of the Middle Ages, to renew its devotion to the care of arts of every period. Within a few decades therefore, papal Rome became a primary center of exchange and study, as well as a seat of the collection of those testimonials of the past that were no longer rejected as being pagan, but that were revisited in an idea of beauty that crossed the borders of the Christian religion or more precisely were re-included,

FIG.1. *Melozzo da Forli,* Sixtus IV Names Bartolomeo Platina Perfect of the Vatican Library. *detached fresco, Vatican Museums.*

through new philosophical ideas, as pre-figurations of the Christian religion and instruments at its service.

This extraordinary season not only inspired the beginnings of the first nucleus of the Vatican collections, it also gave birth to the modern idea of the museum, intended as a collection of a body of artistic works in a specific place to promote the social and cultural growth of the community. The first museum in the world, the Museo Capitolino, was so born, through a simple donation of ancient bronzes made in 1471 by Pope Sixtus IV to the municipality of Rome, as an homage to the great history of the city. The great Della Rovere Pope (fig. 1), creator of the Vatican Library and of the famous Sistine Chapel, thus established papal intervention in the systematic collection of works of ancient art that soon would have the residence next to the Vatican Basilica as its ideal premises.

A few decades later, another Della Rovere Pope, Julius II (1503-1513), would continue the idea of a collection of antiquities that his illustrious predecessor had in some way realized with his symbolic donation to the Roman people. After his election, Julius II gathered some works that were present in the Vatican and a masterpiece he owned, an Apollo which would hence be known as "Apollo del Belvedere" (fig. 2), along the sides of the garden that occupied the courtyard of the small palace of Belvedere, the residence established by Innocent VIII (1484-1492). Some fortunate and clamorous finds—the grandiose Laocoon from the Domus Aurea (fig. 3), the statue of Hercules from Campo dei Fiori—increased the number of items beautifully displayed in the garden of the Belvedere, a real cradle of modern museology. A guidebook to the wonders of Rome of 1510 defined the collection as an "Antiquary of

FIG.2. Apollo del Belvedere, *marble, Vatican Museums.*

FIG. 4. Torso del Belvedere, *marble, Vatican Museums.*

the masters of the late Renaissance in their study of the ancient masterpieces, nourishing the classical ideals of the Parnassus of Raphael's Stanze and inspiring the visions of Michelangelo in the vaulted ceiling of the Sistine Chapel.

The papacy of another Medici, Clement VII (1523-1534), must be remembered for the arrival at the Belvedere of the famous "Torso" of an ancient statue (fig.4) that would be studied by every artist of the sixteenth century. It should also be commended for the serious work of "philological" restoration and completion to which the pope committed the great sculptor of Italian Mannerism, the Servite friar Giovannangelo Montorsoli. (Montorsoli was

Statues" (F. Albertini, *Opusculum de mirabilibus [...] Urbis Romae*, f. 60v) and mentioned the epigraph that, in a peremptory way excluded the "profane people," declaring the collection open to scholars, artists, and men of letters. Under Leo X (1513-1521), a pope of the celebrated Florentine family of the Medici who succeeded Julius II, finds and acquisitions continued with the two statues of the Nile and the Tiber, a statue of Ariadne (believed to be Cleopatra) and of the Tigris, along with many others. Leonardo da Vinci and later Michelangelo attended the Vatican *antiquarium* many times and found inspiration in it. Michelangelo probably completed his statue of the Tigris there. Just as the garden of San Marco in the Florence of Lorenzo il Magnifico with its fragments of Roman statues had inspired artists, the pleasant orange garden of the Belvedere shaped

the author of the outstretched arm of the Laocoon, replaced in the middle of the twentieth century by the original bent arm which was discovered in 1905).

By the middle of the sixteenth century, the exceptional collection of the Belvedere, with its historical nucleus, was complete. The popes of the second half of the century organized the collection with few modifications, although they sometimes removed a few works, either to relocate them within the Vatican complex (for instance, in the "casina" finished by Pius IV in the early 1560s that was decorated with many ancient finds), or to definitively eliminate them as in the case of the statue of Hermes donated by Julius (1550-1555) to the Florentine grand duke Cosimo I that is still in the Uffizi Museum.

A clear indication of the amount of care given the collection, as well as a mark of its crystallization, resides in the fact that Pius IV wanted the statues, housed in large niches in the courtyard, to be protected by great wooden shutters that would defend them from bad weather or involuntary negligence.

He did not realize that in creating these great "tabernacles," as they were called, he had actually contributed to the salvation of the Belvedere collection. In fact, within a few years (those following the Council of Trent of 1545-1563), a different stance behind the refusal of antiquity replaced the humanistic sensibility. This new attitude was generated by the legitimate aspirations of the so-called "catholic reformation" that absorbed the widespread moralizing principles radicalized by the Lutheran reformation, but which in reality was present and active in the entire Christian world of the time. The sainted Pope Pius V (1566-1572) embodied the ideals of that new vision of reality more than anyone else. In his eyes, the great number of pagan statues that decorated the Vatican appeared as a sort of unbearable profanation, and he removed as many statues as possible in any possible way, even through new donations to the Capitol, to the Florence of the Medici, to Roman and foreign cardinals and even to the emperor Maximilian II of Habsburg.

The great museum of antiquities,

FIG.3. Laocoon *from the Domus Aurea, marble, Vatican Museums.*

into which the Vatican had been converted in such a short time, was therefore even more quickly despoiled by the zeal of the sainted pope. The casina of Pius IV now stood bare and unadorned, the courtyards and rooms of the papal palace stripped of every statue. Only the tabernacles in the garden of the Belvedere continued to preserve the few surviving stautes of the first Museum of the Vatican from a paradoxically "involuntary" negligence.

The niches of Belvedere fell into oblivion for more than a century, until the beginning of the eighteenth century when a great pope of the Albani family from Urbino, Clement XI (1700-1721) reopened and replaced the old damaged shutters, restored the statues, and encouraged a new collection of historical and epigraphic documents (called the Museo Ecclesiastico) that would .be housed in the same glorious courtyard and nearby areas. The reason for the failure of that undertaking is not known; however, before the end of the papacy of Pope Clement, the collections of the new Museum were suddenly interrupted and dispersed. After constructing a new large gallery that closed the arcades of a section of the immense courtyard by Bramante between the Apostolic Palace and the small palace of the Belvedere, Clement XII (1730-1740) relocated the spectacular collection of two hundred Greek figurative vases (termed "Etruscan" from

Above: FIG. 5. *Recently restored walnut cabinets in the Museo Cristiano, first installed in the 18th century. Vatican Museums.*

Right: FIG.6. *Octagonal garden courtyard redesigned in the 18th century during the papacy of Clement XIV. Vatican Museums.*

the context of their discovery), originally conceived as ornaments for the wooden cabinets where the manuscripts of the Vatican Library were kept, along with other collections of antiquities.

The real turning point for the collections of the Vatican Museums, however, was marked by the papacy of Benedict XIV Lambertini (1740-1758), a man of extraordinary culture and the creator of many institutions that reinvigorated the intellectual life of eighteenth-century Rome. Under his direction, the Clementine Gallery of the Library filled with documents and works of art from the first centuries of Christianity due, above all, to the acquisition of private

collections that, combined with Etruscan vases and other artistic objects, were seen as a true and real "Vatican Museum" (or so it was defined on plaque in 1749.) The spaces of the Galleria grew ever more inadequate as it coexisted with the library and the ever-increasing collections. The arrival of the great early Christian collection donated by Francesco Vettori in 1756 offered the occasion for the creation of a new renovated museum, the "Museo Cristiano" (Christian Museum), organized in an expressly decorated space—always falling within the Library's jurisdiction—and left to the direction of Vettori himself. Golden glasses and oil lamps, medals and cameos, medieval tablets and liturgical objects, "Etruscan" vases and the fronts of sarcophagi, detached on purpose to hang on the walls, crowded the palace. Splendid walnut cabinets—that the Museums have just restored (fig. 5)—housed the objects in a unity of rare beauty that the following dispersions and rationalizations of the display only allow us to imagine.

Only a few years later, in 1767, Clement XIII (1758-1769) removed the "pagan" works from the end of the Clementine Gallery to create the new Museo Profano (Profane Museum), established for the "preservation of the monuments of Roman antiquity" as the dedicatory inscription declares.

For papal Rome, the eighteenth century was not only the century of the rebirth of the Vatican collections, but also, unfortunately, a period of the continuous dispersion of many private collections that noble families had spent centuries developing, often abetted by local antique dealers for foreign buyers despite the severe long-standing laws that limited the export of artwork. It was in this context that the Franciscan Clement XIV (1769-1774) began his papacy. Preoccupied by the impoverishment of the artistic heritage of the city, he began acquiring works destined for exportation, collecting a large quantity of precious objects in the Vatican that would eventually contribute to the creation of a new, grandiose museum, the first museum in the world created with the scientific intentions and criteria of modern museology. Giambattista Visconti, named "Commissary of the Antiquities," represented the soul of the new institution and directed the work of architects Alessandro Dori and, above all, Michelangelo Simonetti. The space chosen for the collection was that of the old Belevedere of Innocent, surrounding the pulsing heart of the garden which still housed the statues placed there in the sixteenth century. The loggia that opened onto the north side of the garden that had previously been closed was transformed into a Galleria delle Statue (Gallery of Statues), marked and animated by elegant *serliane*

with columns of polychrome marbles. The other rooms of the fifteenth century apartment were readapted to the organization of the new museum. An attempt was made to preserve the old decorative apparatus through the restoration of paintings, to respect the volumetry of spaces, and to conserve the small chapel of San Giovanni, frescoed by Mantegna, to the west of the Galleria delle Statue. The pinnacle of the Clementine intervention on the spaces of the Belvedere was in the reconfiguration of the garden courtyard that was redesigned by Simonetti in an octagonal form with lively neoclassic lines and terminated before the death of the pope who affixed an inscription still visible there today (fig. 6). The last years of his papacy were marked by a careful and serious purchasing campaign, directed by Visconti, that filled the expository spaces with many very important masterpieces (the Jupiter of Casa Verospi, the marble biga of the church of San Marco, the Eros of Centocelle, the gigantic Juno, etc.).

The museum initiated by Clement took on the name Museo Pio-Clementino with the coming of Pope Pius VI Braschi (1775-1799), who had already served as an advisor in the creation of the Museum and treasurer for his predecessor. Pius VI continued to organize the new Vatican museum with renewed enthusiasm: he decided to transfer the entrance of the museum to the end of the Galleria Clementina and the Museo Profano of the Library, renovating an old existing staircase and creating new grandiose spaces inspired by the architecture of ancient Rome, the masterpieces of the early Roman neoclassicism, and the stirring sources of the grand European museums of the eighteenth century. Thus was created in the 1780s through the labor of Simonetti, the new stairs that took his name and that rivaled, if not in grandiosity then at least in formal elegance, the other neoclassic masterpiece, the stairs of the Reggia di Caserta, by Vanvitelli, of some decades before. From there, one could access the Sala a Croce Greca (the Room of the Greek Cross) and further on the Sala delle Muse (the Room of the Muses), both of which were derived from the models of imperial spas; these two rooms were connected in the large Sala Rotonda (Round Room), the real masterpiece of Simonetti, inspired by the Pantheon of Adrian, as well as the great

Above Right: FIG. 7. *The Clementine Statue Gallery, extended in the late 18th century during the papacy of Pius VI. Vatican Museums.*
Right: FIG. 8. *The Etruscan Museum, opened in 1838 by Pope Gregorius XVI. Vatican Museums.*

late ancient circular mausoleums. The new architectonic complex was connected through the Sala delle Muse, ornate with portraits of ancient philosophers, orators, and poets, to the old small palace of the Belvedere, further renovated with the creation of the Sala degli Animali (Room of the Animals), that enlarged a smaller room formerly dedicated to the Torso, and the extension of the Clementine Galleria delle Statue, that unfortunately sacrificed the small chapel by Bramante that had previously spared (Fig.7).

The Museo PioClementino was complete: it was embellished by mosaic floors from Ancient Rome, granite Egyptian telamons, the two enormous porphyry sarcophagi of Helena and Constantine, and many other works (such as the Apollo Sauróktonos and Myron's Discobolus) that, while the re-

FIG. 9. *Athlete, Roman marble copy, probably after a bronze original c. 330 B.C. by Lysippus, Vatican Museums.*

FIG. 10. *Augusta of Prima Porta, c. 20 B.C. marble, Vatican Museums.*

Ennio Quirino. Between 1788 and 1790, a Galleria dei Quadri (Painting Gallery) for the paintings scattered amongst the Vatican palaces was also constructed.

However, a new, insidious danger for the great collection was at the gates: the French Revolution. The tense relationship between the papacy and the revolutionary government of Napoleon Bonaparte led to the invasion of the Papal States (1796) and concluded with an armistice signed in Tolentino, in the Marche region, that provided, among other things, for the transfer of five hundred manuscripts and one hundred works of art, to France, to the Louvre in Paris that had recently been baptized with the new name, Musée Napoléon.

Between April and July 1797 (and then again in 1801), more than one hundred masterpieces left Rome by sea

structuring work was proceeding, were acquired for the collection. In 1786, the creation of a decentralized crossing space, the hall called of the Quattro Cancelli (Four Gates), the work of architect Camporese, was inspired, although in reduced form, by his reverent admiration of the volumetry and the forms of Simonetti's Rotunda. The pope also oversaw the reorganization and enlargement of the collections of the Library (especially the profane section) and promoted the publication of a short guidebook to his great Museum as well as a real systematic catalogue in seven volumes of the collection edited by Giambattista Visconti and later by Visconti's son

and river for the French capital city where they arrived one year later. The main masterpieces mentioned along with many others, the most famous paintings hailing from Rome and the other papal cities, were welcomed by a jubilant crowd as war trophies. In 1798, the officials at the service of the French treasurer Haller, came to take more manuscripts and works of art, and covertly filled their pockets with the priceless glyphic collection of the Library. Meanwhile, the harassed Pius VI left Rome and went first to Florence and then to Valenza, where he died in 1799.

The conclave for the election of Pius VII Chiaramonti (1800-1823) was held in Venice, far from occupied Rome. Not much later, the new pope was able to go back to his seat, abandoned by the French who were suffering the first scorching defeats on the European battlefields. The Museo Pio-Clementino appeared dramatically desolate, with empty bases and frames, filled with casts created in haphazard manner under the direction of Pius VI before the removal of the works. The new pope nominated famous sculptor Antonio Canova to the title of "Inspector for the Fine Arts" and the two attempted to fill the gaps in the collections with new acquisitions and excavations, while also making harsher laws against the export of works of art. However, the number of the new acquisitions grew at such a rate that soon the spaces of the Museo Pio-Clementino were filled and the pontiff thought it advisable to create a new museum that was named after him: Chiaramonti. It occupied the gallery opposite the Clementine gallery of the Library from whence the rich collection of inscriptions of Clement XIV was moved.

Meanwhile, with the fall of Napoleon, the Congress of Vienna (1815) sanctioned the restitution of the works of art appropriated from states occupied by the revolutionaries. Pius VII made Canova responsible for the negotiations and the latter immediately went to Paris to recover the numerous works, despite the resistance of the French government that appealed by referring to the agreement signed by Pius VI in Tolentino. Only the threat of an English military intervention broke the deadlock, and the first works would leave by land on October 25, defying the severe climatic conditions, especially in the crossing of the Alps, when the case containing the *Laocoon* slipped due to ice and fell, causing serious damage to the work. However, Canova's attempts to recover the works were not entirely successful: more than half of the five hundred works that had left Rome and the Papal States (excluding the library patrimony) remained in Paris.

The return of works of art to their displays in the Vatican, like the famous statues in the octagonal courtyard, once again rendered the spaces insufficient. Thus the construction of the so-called Braccio Nuovo (New Wing) (1816-1822), that cut through the long court of Bramante, after the creation of the cross-wise wing of the Library willed by Sixtus V in 1587, was decided. The

FIG. 12. *Caravaggio,* The Disposition from the Cross, *c. 1600, oil on canvas, Vatican Museums.*

pope also ordered that the paintings that had returned to Rome, despite originally hailing from other cities of the State, should remain in the Pinacoteca Vaticana. The Pinacoteca Vaticana, situated in the fourteenth-century apartment of Alexander VI Borgia overlooking the opposite side of the great courtyard of the Belvedere in respect to the small palace of Innocent, was later transferred to the third floor of the Vatican Logge in the Apostolic Palace, and moved again to the Galleria degli Arazzi (Tapestry Gallery) under Pius VIII (1829-1830). New laws instituted by the Papal States guaranteed more important acquisitions including the *Giustiniani Athena*, the fresco of the Aldobrandini Wedding, and the numerous "clay seals" destined to the Library. Between 1818 and 1819, particularly precious finds which would represent the core of the Museo Gregoriano Egizio arrived from Egypt. The acquisitions quickly followed one another, filling any space available in the immense Vatican complex.

One of the last spaces available, the apartment of the librarian Cardinal de Zelada set up at the end of the eighteenth century, was finally occupied by the new Museo Etrusco, called Gregoriano, and was opened by Gregorius XVI (1831-1846) in 1838 (fig. 8). It housed the collection of vases found in the Etruscan necropoleis and many other objects, including the famous bronze statue of Mars found in Todi in 1835 and the exceptional tomb furnishings discovered in southern Etruria (such as those of the famous Regolini-Galassi tomb in Cerveteri) whose fame spread through Europe. Another "Gregorian" museum, the Egyptian one, was founded in 1839 following the progress of Egyptology and the foundation of analogous institutions in Turin and Florence. It filled the spaces behind the large niche with the Pio-Clementino, transferred there from the courtyard of the old Saint Peter's in the seventeenth century.

However, as the collections, especially that of ancient Greco-Roman works, were still growing, the pope decided to place the new acquisitions in the papal palace of the Lateran, the sixteenth century successor of the medieval Patriarchio, the old residence of the popes. Once the building was restored and organized, the new Museo Gregoriano Profano was opened to the public in 1844 with the exhibit of the new acquisitions along with objects from the Vatican (in an attempt to reorganize the overcrowded spaces), a few early Christian monuments, and a new painting gallery displaying modern works and copies of ancient ones.

FIG. 13. *Raphael,* The Transfiguration *c. 1518, tempera and oil on wood panel, Vatican Museums.*

FIG. 11. *An illustration of the Museo Pio Cristiano at the Lateran Palace, opened in 1854 by Pope Pius IX to display early Christian art and artifacts. Vatican Museums.*

During the papacy of Pius IX (1846-1878) that continued for almost the entire second half of the nineteenth century, inestimable masterpieces were added to the collections: the athlete of the Lysippus school (in Greek, apoxyómenos) (fig. 9), the Augustus from Prima Porta (fig. *10*), and the gigantic Hercules found in Campo dei Fiori. However, the pope, who considered himself a new Damasus (the pontiff who, in the fourth century, had embellished and cared for the tombs of the martyrs), is credited with the substantial growth in the papal collections of the artistic creations of the early centuries of Christianity. He established a

"Commission of Sacred Archaeology" that would study and excavate the early Christian cemeteries of Rome, and finally, in 1854, he opened the Museo Pio Cristiano at the Lateran(fig. 11), which was destined to become the most important collection of its kind in the world. The new museum was organized by the Jesuit father Giuseppe Marchi and his best pupil, Giovan Battista de Rossi, the real father of modern Christian Archaeology and excavator of almost all the Roman catacombs (some hidden for more than a thousand years) who brought to light extraordinary artistic finds of the first Christian believers: golden oil lamps and glass, statues, sarcophagi, objects of daily life, and exceptionally preserved frescoes. The objects that could not be kept on the site were transferred, if they were of minor dimensions, to the Museo Sacro della Biblioteca. Otherwise, especially in the case of the sarcophagi, the works were moved to the Museo Cristiano of the Lateran.

At the beginning of the twentieth century, under the papacy of sainted Pope Pius X (1903-1914), the exciting discovery of early medieval reliquaries kept in the chapel of *Sancta Sanctorum* in the Lateran enriched the collections of the Museo della Biblioteca with inestimable treasures (like the bejeweled Cross and the reliquaries of Pope Paschal I). The Library relinquished its collection of paintings of "primitive" Italian painters to the renovated Painting Gallery, marvelously enlarged with adequate, spacious rooms on the floor below the Library (1909). The continuous acquisitions and the desire for an expositive space worthy of the extraordinary painting collection (from Giotto to Raphael and Caravaggio) (figs. 12-13) led to the idea of constructing a new great building connected to the Museum by the hall of the Quattro Cancelli that was realized a few years later, in 1932, under Pius XI (1922-1939). It is to this pope that we owe the institution of the important Museo Missionario Etnologico (Missionary Ethnologic Museum) in the Lateran Palace that opened in 1927 as well as the creation of the new entrance on the Viale Vaticano, with the innovative helicoidal double flight staircase (1932).

After the parenthesis of World War II, acquisitions and expositive improvements continued, and in 1957, a small modern section of the Pinacoteca was created, the first nucleus of the greater enterprise of the papacy of Paul VI (1963-1978), and testimonial to the attention to the world and to "modernity" that intersected with the Church during the post-war period and set the stage for the Council. The decision of Pope John XXIII (1958-1963) to relocate the seat of the pope, the Bishop of Rome, to the Lateran palace, close to the cathedral of San

FIG. 14. *Papal Historical Museum, opened in 1973. Vatican Museums.*

Giovanni, inspired the transfer of the museums housed there (Gregoriano Profano, Pio Cristiano and Etnologico) to the Vatican. They were accommodated in a new building erected behind that of the Pinacoteca, a large part of which was underground. In 1970, after a few years of preparation, the Museo Gregoriano Profano and the Pio Cristiano were opened, and in 1973, the new display of the Etnologico was open. In the same year, a new Museo Storico Pontificio (Papal Historical Museum) was opened along with a large new section devoted to the Collezione d'Arte Religiosa Moderna e Contemporanea (Collection of Early Modern and Modern Religious Art), rich in masterpieces, a product of the Council's attention to the "signs of the times" (fig. 14). Among the new possessions was the important Astarita collection of Etruscan finds (1967-1968), acquired thirty years after the donation of the other great collection by Giacinto Guglielmi.

In these recent years under the papacy of John Paul II (elected in 1978 and still happily reigning), the life of the Museums has been marked on the one hand by a large number of restorations that reached their climax in the grandiose enterprise of the Sistine Chapel (fig. 15); and on the other hand by the fact that the Museums have promoted or participated in important exhibits all over the world. They have exhibited their treasures in order to open themselves even more fully to the society and culture of the modern world, spreading a message of peace and collaboration among people. The great Jubilee of the year 2000 also witnessed the construction of a new impressive entry (fig. 16), whose "new door" was opened for the first time by the pope – in the tradition of those pontiffs who were more personally and generously connected to the museums. The pope has equipped the Vatican Museums with welcoming structures worthy of one the greatest museums in the world, including a gallery already used for important temporary exhibits.

The steps taken outside and, at the same time, the constant improvement of the "inside" of the Museums are indicative, we believe, of the current directive lines we are pursuing with enthusiasm and along which we imagine the Vatican Museums as a bright mirror of the life of the Church itself, and of the devotion to cultivating the gifts and fragments of beauty received, and at the same time, to sharing them with everyone in order for the Christian message of hope and peace to reach "the uttermost part of the earth" (*Acts of the Apostles* 1, 8).

—Francesco Buranelli

Above: FIG. 16. *A new entry to the Vatican Museums constructed in 2000. Vatican Museums.*
Left: FIG. 15. *The Sistine Chapel, ceiling completed in 1512 by Michelangelo.* Last Judgement *completed in 1541. Vatican Museums.*

In the plans of 1323, Fra' Paolino da Venezia outlined the centers of the Roman settlement within the Aurelian walls and detailed them in such a way to convey the density of population of the quarters of Borgo, Trastevere, Ripa and of the built area in the Tiber's bend.[1] An extremely modern vision of the city, that was very similar to the great cartographic views of the fifteenth and sixteenth centuries, already existed then, and was in clear contrast with the official images of the Rome of the fourteenth century (fig. 1) which tended to identify the city by its more significant monuments and churches: Palazzo Senatorio, Torre delle Milizie, Pantheon, Castel Sant'Angelo.[2] The medieval urban core, as represented by Fra' Paolino da Venezia, had developed within an area bounded by the ancient Via *Recta* (now Via dei Coronari) that closed the city to the north near Sant'Angelo bridge and by the ancient Via *Lata* (now Via del Corso) that led to the Capitol from the Flaminia gate (now Porta del Popolo) under which, turning east, the road forked entering the Forum or Trastevere, through the Rotto Bridge (fig. 2). The city had moved along the river on the right bank with the Trastevere (which had been widened in the northbound direction in the twelfth century in parallel with the development of

FIG. 1. *Assisi, Upper Basilica of San Francesco, Ytalia by Cimabue (photo © Scala, Florence)*

Borgo) and on the left bank with two older areas of settlement, one located between the Tiber and the northern slopes of the Capitol and the other situated between the Pantheon and the Piazza Navona, that had merged to occupy the river's bend between the eleventh and twelfth centuries.[3]

Borgo had been developing since the ninth century, when Pope Leo IV (848-855) erected a circle of walls to defend the Vatican area, creating the so called 'città leonina' (city of Leo). The contruction of the basilica of Saint Peter's had in fact already radically changed the character of the entire area and became the catalyzing element of the new urban structure. Soon many civil and even more religious buildings would be erected and an entirely new neighborhood would develop. This area, termed "burg," a word of gothic origin, was inhabited especially by foreigners (Saxons, Franks and Lombards) who had founded there their *scholae*,[4] which remained active until the fourteenth and fifteenth centuries. Borgo became then an almost autonomous entity and assumed the form that it would preserve until 1938, with the opening of Via della Conciliazione. However, before the thirteenth century, the Popes did not reside at the Vatican: the official seat of Rome's bishop was, in

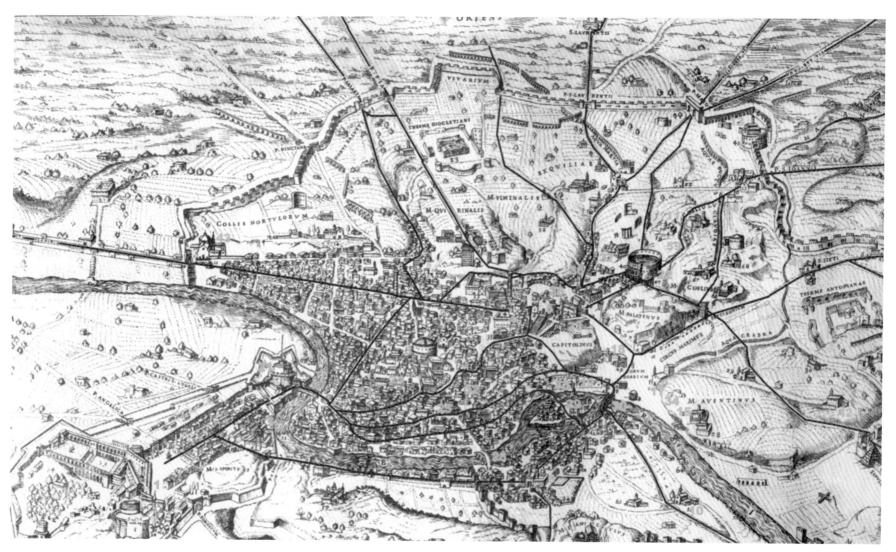

FIG. 2. *Plan of Rome in the Middle Ages. Graphic processing: arch. P. Di Nezio.*
On the plan by Cartaro (1575) the medieval routes (in red) and the main medieval building (in blue)
have been highlighted. 1) San Pietro; 2)San Giovanni in Laterano; 3) Santa Maria ad Martires
(Pantheon); 4) San Marco; 5) Church and hospital of Santo Spirito in Sassia; 6) Santa Maria in
Aracoeli (Santa Maria in Capitolio); 73 San Lorenzo; 8) Santa Maria Maggiore; 9) Santa Maria in
Trastevere; 10) San Biagto (San Francesco a Ripa); 11) San Clemente; 12) Santi Quattro Coronati;
13) Santa Croce in Gerusalemme; 14) Santo Stefano Rotondo; 15) Santa Sabina; 16) Santi Giovanni
e Paolo; 171 Santa Maria in Cosmedin; 18) San Giorgio al Velabro; 19) San Nicola in Carcere; 20)
Sant'Agnese; 21) Sant'Angelo Castle; 22) Colosseum; 23) Capitol; 24) piazza Navona; 25) Campo
dei Fiori; 26) Roman Forum; 27) Sant'Angelo bridge; 28) Valentiniano bridge; 29) Quattro Capi and
Cestio bridges; 30) 'Rotto' bridge (Santa Marial); 31) Orsini complex at Monte Giordano; 32) fortress of
the Orsini on the Theater of Pompeus; 33) fortress of the Savelli on the Theater of Marcellus; 34) Savelli
stronghold on the Aventine; 35) tower of the Milizie; 36) tower of the Conti; 37) fortress of the
Annibaldi and church of San Pietro in Vincoli; 38) hospital of San Giovanni; 39) hospital of San
Giovanni in Formis; 40) hospital of San Giacomo in Augusta; 41) San Sisto vecchio; 42) San Saba; 43)
Santa Maria del Popolo.

fact, starting with the age of Constantine, the Lateran. Saint Peter's was considered only a basilica 'fuori le mura' (outside the walls), constructed with the goal of venerating the tomb of the apostle, and related to the cemetery that had developed around it. Pope Nicholas III (1277-1280) became the first pontiff to house his court permanently within the Vatican. Following this event, it became necessary to widen the city walls, to construct crenellation, and to build the 'Passetto di Borgo' to connect the palace with the Castel Sant'Angelo in order to guarantee the safety of the pope. During the residence of the popes in Avignon (1377), when the Roman senate was compelled to definitely cede the fortress of Sant'Angelo Castle to the church, the 'città leonina' became safe, although struggles, sieges, and assaults ensued around it, and conflicts among the papal, imperial, and communal powers swirled within it.

The city of Rome was tightly bound to Saint Peter's throughout the Middle Ages. Three arteries crossed the constructed center from east to west and converged right on the Sant'Angelo bridge, the first from the Quattro Capi

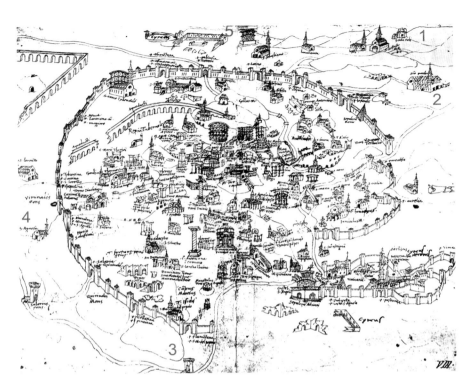

FIG. 4. *Alessandm Strozzi, Drawing, Rome, 1474. 1) abbey of the Tre Fontane; 2) San Paolo; 3) "Mollo" (Milvio) bridge; 4) Sant'Agnese; 5) Capo di Bove (Cecilia Metella).*

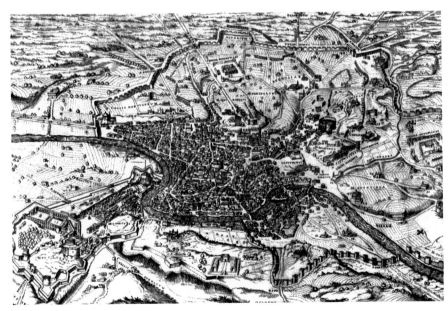

FIG. 3 *Plan of Rome in the Middle Ages. Graphic processing: arch. P. Di Nezio.*

bridge (from the Tiber island), the second from the Rotto bridge through the Ghetto, Giubbonari, and Campo dei Fiori which rejoined the first artery in Via dei Banchi Vecchi, and the third, used by papal processions and pilgrims to traverse the Lateran (that hosted the cathedral of Rome and served as the seat of the ecclesiastical offices and, until Nicholas III, the papal residence) in order to arrive at Saint Peter's passing through the Colosseum, the Capitol, Via delle Botteghe Oscure, Corso Vittorio, and the Via di Parione (Governo Vecchio).[5] Only a few sporadic settlements and churches existed outside this constructed area. Although located off the main circuits, these churches were still served by the old Roman roads as they had been built when the ancient system was still working (fig. 3).

Generally the Roman antiquities had either been incorporated into the urban fabric or abandoned or, as in the case of functional structures like bridges, aqueducts and walls, were still in use. Only in a few cases had they taken on a role of real urban poles: Adrian's mausoleum, like Castel Sant'Angelo, had become the fortified core defending Saint Peter's, Marcello's Theatre represented the defensive bastion for the bridges of the island, and the Capitol, located at the margin of the built-up area, hosted the market on its western slope.

The image of the fourteenth century urban landscape has been returned to us through the subsequent representations of the fifteenth and sixteenth centuries that document a city where the medieval imprint is still very recognizable. Inside the Aurelian walls were large, constructed areas, densely populated and studded with towers, churches, bridges, and ancient monuments, surrounded by a wide belt, 'the uninhabited' area, with only a few houses scattered here and there to mark the way toward the other important pole, the Lateran.[6]

The high towers, emblems of the single noble families, were a characteristic element in the city, and in some cases they are still identifiable in the modern city as remains of the larger complexes of the urban aristocracy. Since the middle of the thirteenth century the upper orders had been divided in *nobiles viri*, representatives of the emerging middle and lower bourgeoisie, and *barones*, members of the powerful Roman families (Orsini, Conti, Annibaldi, Colonna, Savelli) who had replaced the old clans of the Pierleoni and Frangipane.[7] The former were engaged in commercial and judicial activities while also holding ecclesiastical and political offices. The latter instead were represented in large numbers in the curia and were elected alternatively to senatorial offices and the papal throne.[8]

It is obvious then that the towers of the *nobiles viri* had a strong symbolic value rather than simply a defensive function and represented the core of purely urban complexes that, as such, could also be crossed by a road that remained public and could provide services to the community, such as the use of baths and ovens. They were composed of several buildings and open spaces, arranged around the tower owned by the members of the family in such a way that nobody "owning it entirely, could live in it or use it for military purpose against his relatives or neighbors, and on the contrary the possession *pro indiviso* guaranteed concord and unity within the family that identified itself with it."[9]

The complexes of the *nobiles viri* were located in the more populated areas of the city, divided in *rioni* (districts) that became more and more characterized by the coexistence of workshops and the dwellings of nobles, artisans and merchants.[10] Businessmen and small artisans both resided and kept their workshops in

Above: FIG. 5. *Rome, Tower of the Conti (photo © Gabriele Basilico, Milan).*
Right: FIG. 6. *Rome, Tower of the Milizie (photo Lulgl Ghirri).*

Trastevere, and traders had their stalls in the nearby Borgo that became an autonomous district only in 1586.[11] In this living context, characterized exclusively by the presence of *nobiles viri*, traders, and artisans, the presence of the Orsini family was an exception. Although the family belonged with full titles to the class of the *barones*, they had a few houses in Campo dei Fiori, above Pompeus' Theatre, probably to ensure control over the section of the *Via Papalis* toward Saint Peter (fig. 4).

Instead, the same road on the side of the Lateran was guarded by the strongholds of the Conti and Annibaldi families (fig. 5) that, like all the other fortresses of the *barones*, occupied the peripheries of the constructed area, utilizing the high grounds and isolated zones to control the territory.[12] Among these fortresses we can also count the other large urban complex of the Orsini family at Monte Giordano (fig. 6). Those fortresses were defended by walls and were sometimes set up on the ancient monuments themselves, like in the case of the Savelli family who lived in the old theater of Marcellus, but built their "Rocca Savella" (Savelli stronghold) on the Aventino. They proposed a kind of structure (a square fortified enclosure with towers) that had been experimented with in the *Campagna Romana*, for example, on the Via Appia where the castle of Capo di Bove (fig. 7) was built on the mausoleum of Cecilia Metella by the Caetani family. (The Caetani had forcefully stormed onto the scene of the Roman nobility with the election of Boniface VIII Caetani (1294-1303), also acquiring the Milizie castle from the Annibaldi family.)

The power of the *barones* was derived from this tight bond, often through kinship ties, and often with links to the curia and the papacy, as many of their representatives were elected to the papal throne. For example, Innocent III (1198-1216), Gregory IX (1227-1241), and Alexander IV (1254-1261) belonged to the Conti di Segni family; Honorius III (1216-1227) and Honorius IV (1285-1287) to the Savelli line; Nicholas III (1277-1280) to the Orsini clan; and Boniface VIII to the Caetani dynasty. "It is significant that among the barons only three families (the Normanni, the Sant'Eustachio, and the Anguillara) never had a cardinal or a pope. For almost all the others, the propelling element, the determining factor of family greatness can be found instead in the nepotism of a relative elected to the Sacred College or maybe to the papacy."[13] (fig. 8)

These two forces were so tightly connected—*barones* and papacy—that they substantially influenced the life and culture of the city. The *barones*, with their fortified complexes that determined the city planning of Rome, had forcefully secured large urban areas, and, for a short time, faced challenges from Brancaleone degli Andalò, not by chance a foreigner (from Bologna), a senator from 1252 to 1258. The Commune, in fact, was also subject to the pope and for the first half of the thirteenth century it does not appear to have played an active role in Rome's upgrading. The papacy and the curia were the two institutions that restored and built Rome, caring primarily for the religious buildings. In fact, they had intervened in the churches of Santi Sergio e Bacco, San Sisto Vecchio, Santi Giovanni e Paolo, San Saba, San Pietro in Vincoli, and San Lorenzo Fuori le Mura. They played an active role in the completion of the papal palace around 1208; the fortification of the lateran patriarchate and Laurentiopolis;[14] the arcades, bell towers, and cloisters of several churches, as

FIG. 7. *Rome, Capo di Bove (photo © Gabriele Basilico, Milan).*

"by now well studied centripetal practice of settlement that from the outside of the city took them in a few decades to privileged areas located first inside the walls, and then in the heart of the political and economic activities of the different urban centers."[16]

Since 1250, with the opening of the new construction sites of the Franciscan church of Santa Maria in Aracoeli—built on the location of the old Santa Maria in Capitolio—and the city hall, the city's attention moved to the Capitol, where the cultural and political situation had been evolving in an "international" sense because of the presence of foreign personalities in both the senatorial office (Brancaleone degli Andalò from Bologna to Carlo d'Angiò: 1265, 1268-1278, 1281-1284), the papal throne (Urban IV, 1261-1264; Clement IV, 1265-1268; John XXI, 1276-1277; and Martin IV, 1281-1285), and as usual the Roman curia.[17]

well as the organization of hospices and hospitals. Indeed, Pope Innocent III instituted the Hospital of San Spirito in Sassia (1198-1201), to be inserted within the restructuring project of the Vatican area with the construction of the new residence, and that of San Tommaso in Formis at the Celio (fig. 9) while Cardinal Giovanni Colonna formed the first core of the hospital of San Giovanni in 1216.[15] At that time, the new religious Orders also came into play. The Dominicans first settled at San Sisto Vecchio (1219) and then at Santa Sabina on the Aventino (1221). The Cistercians established themselves at Tre Fontane, and the Franciscans were first guests (1219) and then owners (1229) at S. Biagio close to Porta Portese (now San Francesco a Ripa), at San Maria del Popolo, consecrated in 1234, and then finally at Santa Maria in Capitolo (1249) on the Capitoline hill where the new city hall was being built. In Rome as well, the Franciscans accomplished the

Before 1257, the construction of the *palatium novo*, the new city hall, edified on the structure of the ancient *Tabularium*, had begun. However, a fundamental variation characterized the structure: the upturn of the façade gave the new building control over the new constructed areas , not over the Forum.[18] (fig. 10)

From that moment on, construction on the hall continued throughout the century with the addition of a *lobium* at the end of the thirteenth century, the construction of a lateral tower by Boniface VIII in 1300, a restructuring of the fortifications ordered by Cola di Rienzo in 1344, and the building of the new towers of Boniface IX (1389-1404).[19] It is clear, therefore, that despite the departure of the papacy from Rome to Avignon (1305-1377), the pontiffs and the curia continued to care for the city not only in the recovery of religious architecture, but also in the protection of civil and charitable structures. The

Hospital of San Giacomo in Augusta was founded in 1339, but already in 1343 the funds for the restoration of "Ponte Mollo" had to be obtained from the queen of Hungary who was visiting the city.[20] The commissioning was no longer the almost exclusive prerogative of the papacy and curia, although they were always present in some way. Different forces had come into play.

The political situation that had developed in Rome with the departure of the popes had become extremely critical because of the constant struggles between the different *barones* who wanted to control the city (above all the Orsini and Colonna families). They were only weakly opposed by the popular government for short periods.[21] This led to a serious economic crisis, the causes of which were tightly intertwined. The absence of the papacy led to the termination of work at the great construction sites, the departure of the curia caused a large imbalance on the production of goods and services connected to it, and the lack of safety on the roads caused a decrease of the influx of pilgrims, who would later return on the occasion of the 'Jubilee Without the Pope' of 1350.[22]

The baronage, at this point strongly at the head of the Commune, hindered any initiative of the urban orders to preserve their supremacy and maintain control over the political and economic situation, and thus tended to monopolize the flows of money and the purchases of lands and goods.[23]

All these factors inevitably contributed to the rise to power of Cola di Rienzo, first in 1347 and then, for very few months, in 1354. His political program could also seem extremely simplistic, based as it was on order, justice, and peace; however, it also revealed a consistent vision of contemporary society and was presented to the people with great lucidity and attention to public image.[24]

FIG 8. *The Anguillara Building in Trastevere, Rome (photo ©Abbrescia and Santinelli).*

Ephemeral ornaments for parades were therefore more important than a serious architectonic policy for the city, and the only intervention ascribable to Cola di Rienzo in his role as a tribune seems to be the construction of a chapel in the city hall.[25]

Despite the fact that the influence of Cola di Rienzo was very short-lived and the *barones* quickly regained control, the conflicts soon reappeared and led to the popular regime of the *Felice Società dei Balestrieri e Pavesati* that lasted until 1398.

The second half of the fourteenth century was heavily marked not only by economic and political crisis, but also by the plague of 1348 that contributed to a period of great transformation—negative, but in the long run also constructive— caused by the drop in prices, the increase of wages and available land, and the subversion of the entire system.[26]

The last great enterprise of the fourteenth century, the grandiose steps of the Aracoeli, was attributable to the contributions of the people rather than to the commissioning of the popes and the nobles. The steps were erected in 1348 as a votive offering after the plague. The work, executed by Lorenzo di Simone Andreozio as an important point of entry into the church, also changed access to the Capitoline hill that had already witnessed the upturn of the façade of the new hall, connecting the hill more closely with the urban area below. [27]

The last architectonic works of the century were limited to the partial rebuilding or the completion of already existing public structures. After the earthquake of 1349, the collapsed tower bell of San Paolo Fuori le Mura was rebuilt. In 1377, Santa Maria Maggiore was renovated and, with Pope Boniface IX, the Capitol was reinforced.

The city of the late fourteenth century was a metropolis surrounded by an abandoned countryside, as the inhabitants preferred to find shelter within the walls, occupying the wide spaces that had been left empty by then. The city's short-range trades were circumscribed to its immediate environs, and only after the return of the popes would "the foreign dealers" begin to invest again, to enter into contracts, and to conduct business on the Roman market. However, it would take at least a decade after the return of the pope from Avignon before the city would begin to experience economic results due to the reestablishment of the papal court in Rome.[28]

—Paola Rossi

FIG. 9 *Church of San Tommaso in Formis, Rome (photo © Abbrescia and Santinelli).*

END NOTES

[1] Fra' Paolino da Venezia in the two versions of the Vaticana and Marciana: Satirica Historia, Biblioteca Vaticana, Vat. Lat. 1960, fol. 270v; Venice, Biblioteca Marciana, Lat. Z. 399, c. 98.

[2] We refer in particular to the *Bulla Aurea* by Ludwig from Bavaria (1328, Munich, Bayerisches Hauptstaatsarchiv) and the *Ytalia* by Cimabue in the vault of the Evangelists in the upper Basilica of San Francesco in Assisi. On the topic, see Andaloro, 1985, pp. 143-181.

[3] See Krautheimer, 1981, pp. 306-308.

[4] Colonies of foreigners who built their homes, church, and even a cemetery there.

[5] See Krautheimer, 1981, p. 308; Rossi, 1998, pp. 125-126; Santangeli Valenzani, 1998, pp. 145-152.

[6] The image of Rome presented to pilgrims and visitors is well documented in the *Codex Escurialensis* of the end of the fifteenth century (circa 1495) and in the drawings by Marten van Heemskerck, datable to the years 1534-1536 (see H. Egger, ed.), *Codex Escurialensis*, 2 vol., Wien 1905-1906, fol. 56v; 40v; Marten van Heemskerck, Berlin, Kupferstichkabinett, 79D2, fol. 91v, 92r).

[7] The Orsini, the Capocci and the Normanni clans already achieved much prominence by the end of the twelfth century. They were then joined by the Conti and the Annibaldi (thirteenth century) and later by the Colonna, Savelli and Caetani families (fourteenth century). On the topic see Carocci, Venditelli, 2001, pp. 88-99.

[8] "It has been calculated that in the period from 1230 to 1358, the Orsini were elected to that office 50 times, the Annibaldi 28, the Colonna 24, the Conti 17, the Savelli 15, leaving it to other baronal families less than thirty times" (Maire Viguer, 2001, p. 133).

[9] See Bernacchio, 2000, p. 73. On the topic, see also Venditelli, 1989, pp. 216-242, and Hubert, 1990, pp. 169-200.

[10] The term *rione* derives from a corruption of the word *regiones*. Already since 1149, in fact, the city was divided in *contradae*. More *contradae* represented a *regio*, known by the name of the *contradae* by which it was composed, that formed the administrative circumscriptions. Since the thirteenth century, the *regio* replaced the *contrada* as administrative circumscription; in 1220 there were 12 *regiones* that grew to 13 at the beginning of the fourteenth century. The borders were, however, never well defined. On the subject, see Hubert, 2001, pp. 176-177.

[11] On the topic, see Krautheimer, 1981, pp. 342-343.

[12] The fortress of the Conti, organized around the tower that still survives today, was built by Innocent III (1198-1216) for his brother Riccardo. They had other estates in the area of the Militiae, where, during the thirteenth century, a system of control was built that hinged upon the imposing tower of the Milizie, on that of Grillo and that of the Colonna. The Annibaldi, blood relations of the Colonna, were influential in the zone around the Colosseum, that had belonged to the Frangipane in the twelfth century. On the topic see Righetti Tosti-Croce, 1991, pp. 131-143; Bernacchio, 2000, pp. 75-78.

[13] See Carocci, Venditelli, 2001, p. 94.

[14] On the interventions in Rome in the first half of the thirteenth century and on the fortified citadel of Laurentiopolis, destroyed at the end of the sixteenth century, see Pistilli, 1991, pp. 1-71: 24. We refer to this study also for the previous bibliography.

[15] On the topic, see Righetti Tosti-Croce, 1999, p. 90.

[16] See Righetti Tosti-Croce, 1999, p. 91.

[17] On the topic, see Righetti Tosti-Croce, 1991, pp. 80-95; Righetti Tosti-Croce, 2000, p. 21.

FIG. 10. *Rome, Palazzo Senatorio (photo © Gabriele Basilico, Milan).*

[18] On the topic, see Righetti Tosti-Croce, 1991, p. 80.
[19] In 1344, Cola di Rienzo held the office of notary of the Camera Capitolina and began his electoral campaign. On the topic, see Marie Viguer, 2001, p. 148.
[20] On the topic see, Righetti Tosti-Croce, 1996, pp. 93-128; Righetti Tosti-Croce, 1999, pp. 91-95.
[21] On the topic see, Carocci, Venditelli, 2001, pp. 99-108.
[22] On the situation in Rome in the first half of the fourteenth century and at the moment of the Jubilee of 1350, see Moreno, 1999, pp. 235-240. To make even more clear the contrast between the situation in Rome in the late fourteenth century and the levels of achievement attained by the city at the time of Boniface VIII, we also want to mention the institution of the *Studium Urbis* in 1303.
[23] On the topic, see Carocci, Venditelli, 2001, p. 103.
[24] A detailed report of the conduct of Cola di Rienzo appears in the *Cronica* by the Anonymous Roman who described the scenographic stage of the places of public ceremonies and the constant use by the tribune of allegorical paintings to illustrate the Roman situation to the people. On the topic, see Marie Viguer, 2001, pp. 146-151.
[25] On the topic, see Righetti, 1999, pp. 94-95.
[26] See Carocci, Venditelli, 2001, p. 108.
[27] On the topic, see Righetti Tosti-Croce, 1999, p. 95.
[28] See Carocci, Venditelli, 2001, pp. 108-116.

REFERENCES

Andaloro M., *Ancora una volta sull'Ytalia di Cimabue*, in "Arte Medievale," II, 1985, pp. 143-181
Bernacchio N., *La città turrita*, in *Bonifacio VIII e il suo tempo; anno 1300 il primo giubileo*, cat. Mostra 12 apr.-16 lugl. 2000, Milano 2000, pp. 73-78
Bonifacio VIII e il suo tempo; anno 1300 il primo giubileo, a cura di M. Righetti Tosti-Croce, cat. mostra 12 apr.-16 lugl. 2000, Milano 2000
Carocci S., *Baroni di Roma. Dominazioni signorili e lignaggi aristocratici nel Duecento e nel primo Trecento*, Roma 1993a
Carocci S., *Baroni in città. Considerazioni sull'insediamento e i diritti urbani della grande nobiltà*, in *Roma nei secoli XIII e XIV, Cinque saggi*, Roma 1993b
Carocci S., *Il nepotismo nel Medioevo. Papi, cardinali e famiglie nobili*, Roma 1999
Carocci S., *Una nobiltà bipartita. Rappresentazioni sociali e lignaggi preminenti a Roma nel Duecento e nella prima metà del Trecento*, in "Bullettino dell'Istituto storico italiano per il Medio Evo e Archivio Muratoriano," 95 (1989), pp. 71-122
Carocci S., Vendittelli M., *Società ed economia (1050-1420)*, in *Roma medievale. Storia di Roma dall'antichità a oggi*, a cura di A. Vauchez, Roma 2001, pp. 71-116
Case e torri medioevali a Roma. Documentazione, storia e sopravvivenza di edifici medioevali nel tessuto urbano di Roma, I, Roma 1998, pp. 3-98; 297-341
Hubert E., *Espace urbain et habitat à Rome du Xe siècle à la fin du XIIIe siècle*, Roma 1990
Hubert E., *L'organizzazione territoriale e l'urbanizzazione*, in *Roma medievale. Storia di Roma dall'antichità a oggi*, a cura di A. Vauchez, Roma 2001 pp. 159-186
Krautheimer R., *Roma. Profilo di una città 312-1308*, Roma 1981
Maire Viguer J.-C., *Il Comune Romano*, in *Roma medievale. Storia di Roma dall'antichità a oggi*, a cura di A. Vauchez, Roma 2001, pp. 117-157
Morello G., *Il Giubileo senza papa*, in *Romei e Giubilei, Il pellegrinaggio medievale a San Pietro (350-1350)*, a cura di M. D'Onofrio, cat. mostra Roma Palazzo Venezia, 29 ott.-26 feb. 2000, Milano 1999, pp. 235-240
Pistilli P.F., *L'architettura a Roma nella Prima Metà del Duecento (1198-1254)*, in *Roma nel Duecento. L'arte nella città dei papi da Innocenzo III a Bonifacio VIII*, a cura di A.M. Romanini, Torino 1991, pp. 1-71
Righetti Tosti-Croce M., *Appunti sull'architettura a Roma tra Due e Trecento*, in "Arte Medievale", II, 1985, pp. 183-193
Righetti Tosti-Croce M., *Architettura tra Roma, Napoli e Avignone nel Trecento*, in *Roma, Napoli, Avignone. Arte di curia, arte di corte 1300-1377*, a cura di A. Tomei, Torino 1996, pp. 93-128
Righetti Tosti-Croce M., *L'Architettura tra il 1254 e il 1308*, in *Roma nel Duecento. L'arte nella città dei papi da Innocenzo III a Bonifacio VIII*, a cura di A.M. Romanini, Torino 1991 pp. 73-143
Righetti Tosti-Croce M., *Roma anno 1300*, in *Bonifacio VIII e il suo tempo; anno 1300 il primo giubileo*, cat. Mostra 12 apr.-16 lugl. 2000, Milano 2000, pp. 21-23
Righetti Tosti-Croce M., *s.v. Roma, architettura secoli 13°-14°*, in Enciclopedia dell'Arte Medievale. Istituto della Enciclopedia Italiana , vol. X, Roma 1999, pp. 90-96
Roma medievale. Storia di Roma dall'antichità a oggi, a cura di A. Vauchez, Roma 2001
Roma nel Duecento. L'arte nella città dei papi da Innocenzo III a Bonifacio VIII, a cura di A.M. Romanini, Torino 1991
Romei e Giubilei, Il pellegrinaggio medievale a San Pietro (350-1350), a cura di M. D'Onofrio, cat. mostra Roma Palazzo Venezia, 29 ott.-26 feb. 2000, Milano 1999
Rossi P., "*Via Papae, via Papalis*," in *Corso Vittorio Emanuele II tra urbanistica e archeologia. Storia di uno sventramento*, cat. mostra 6 feb.-29 mar. 98, Napoli 1998, pp. 125-126
Santangeli Valenzani R., *Arcus Nervale, templum Jani, arcus Aureae: l'ordo di Benedetto Canonica e la topografia dell'area dei fori imperiali nel medioevo*, in Bullettino della Commissione Archeologica Comunale di Roma, XCIX, 1998, pp. 145-152
Vendittelli M., *La famiglia Curtabraca. Contributo alla storia della nobiltà romana del Duecento*, in "Mélanges de l'Ecole française de Rome, Moyen Age," 101 (1989), I, pp. 177-272

FIG. 1. *Extract of the Plan of Rome by L. Bufalini (1551).*
(All figures in this chapter supplied by the author.)

Beginning with the fifteenth century the large area of the *Foro Boario*—so called after the name of the historic cattle market held on the same site during ancient times—represents the external margin to the south of the constructed zone. The rural appearance of this space that so excited and surprised transalpine visitors because of the mixture of the sacred and profane, flocks of sheep and goats, archaeological areas, barns, and monuments, extended to the side of the Capitoline hill, called for this reason *Monte Caprino* (Mount Goat).

Near the southeastern sector of the hill is the church of San Nicola in Carcere, so called for the historic presence of the *carceres* (the cages for the start of horse races) of the Circus Maximus near the circular temple dedicated to Hercules Victor. The church, consecrated in 1128, stands in the area of the *Foro Olitorio* (vegetable market), on a complex of three Roman temples of the beginning of the second century A.D. dedicated to Janus, Juno, and Spes.[1] The three sacred buildings, between the *Pietas* Temple to the north, where the Theater of Marcellus would later rise, and the area of

the *Portus Tiberinus* to the south, were incorporated in the church that occupied the area of the central temple, that of Juno, and the spaces between it and the two lateral ones. The medieval building—developing in this way among Roman structures and columns that are still clearly visible on the outside on the long sides today—stood in a right angle position to one of the main roads of the time that, coming from the cathedral of Saint Peter, passed the Campo Marzio and the Portico d'Ottavia, turned around the curve of the Theater of Marcellus and headed south outside the built-up area.

In reconstructing medieval city-planning, we are not helped by the representations of the time that portray Rome according to stereotypical models: the circular city bordered by walls (see the essay by P. Rossi, fig. 2) that contained the graphic representation of the seven hills, the river and the main monuments.[2] Only from the second half of the sixteenth century did the city's iconographic documentation begin to take a more scientific character closer to its image in reality; besides the monuments, the morphologic features of the urban lay-out and of the different building typologies (monuments, houses, streets, squares, etc.) are represented.

Particularly useful for the reading of the area is the plan drawn by Bufalini in 1551 (fig. 1), because, more technical than those still beautiful perspective views of the sixteenth century, as well as original and full of information, it presents at the same time the indication of the blocks and the orographic state of the city.

In the detail of the area of interest, one can clearly note the sharp difference between the large flat area of the *Foro Boario*—where one can recognize the isolated Temple of Portuno, that of Hercules Victor, Santa Maria in Cosmedin, and the Arch of Janus—and the articulated urban fabric beyond the line that from the Santa Maria bridge (Ponte Rotto) reaches San Giorgio al Velabro. In the plan, one can note distinctly how the author graphically highlights the two imposing elevations of the area: the Capitoline hill with the mass of tufaceous rock circumscribed by the buildings leaning against it, and the Theatre of Marcellus. These two great volumes, emerging from the overall structure of the built-up area, represented the physical limit of the expansion of the city southwards and, with their close and opposed curves, generated a narrow passage in which the roads coming out from the built-up area towards the *Foro Boario* merged.

The structure of the urban fabric, conditioned by the Capitoline hill and the Theatre of Marcellus, is clearly perceivable also in the subsequent plan by Du Pérac of 1577 (fig. 2) and, with greater evidence, in that by Antonio Tempesta of 1593 (fig. 3). In the two representations in perspective, one can note how, beyond that junction, in which the theatre plays the role of hinge in the urban

FIG. 2. *Extract of "Nova Urbis Romae descriptio" by E. Du Perac (1577).*

conformation of the sector, immediately after *Piazza Montanara*, the road structure widens, passing before the little square of San Nicola in Carcere, and continues in an homogenous way as far as it intercepts the course of the Santa Maria Bridge, and loses afterwards its urban connotation, dispersing in the *Foro Boario*. In this tract, the buildings that survived the decline of the area—subsequent to the conspicuous gathering of noble residences of the medieval age—were, besides the church of San Nicola in Carcere, Santa Maria del Portico, San Salvatore del Portico, the houses of the Pierleoni, that of the Crescenzi and the church of Sant'Omobono, almost all recognizable in the cited cartography.

Beyond those last offshoots of the constructed area, barns, granaries, vegetable gardens, the constant presence of flocks, ox carts, and mills, lent the zone a romantic and fascinating connotation, definitely not comparable to the other great European cities of the time.

This rural appearance, stronger around Piazza Bocca della Verità, remained unchanged throughout the seventeenth and eighteenth centuries, and was radically modified only at the end of the nineteenth century by the new role that the city took as the capital of the Kingdom of Italy.

The years under the Napoleonic government marked the reversal of the trend of immobility that had lasted for centuries. In particular, Count Camillo De Tournon, Prefect of Rome from 1809 to 1814, was the protagonist of a social and economic reorganization of the city, and above all was responsible for the attempt to transform the old city center by "enhancing" the monumental elements by isolating them and widening the road network for the creation of perspective axes.[3] Without the defeat of Napoleon, De Tournon would probably

FIG. 3. *Extract of the "Plan of Rome" by A. Tempesta (1593).*

have become the first city planner of Rome, and could have achieved results akin to those completed a few years later in Paris by the demolitions of Haussmann.[4]

Beginning with the Capitol, as seat of their government, the French started a series of modifications for the "liberation" and isolation of monumental elements: for our zone, the Temple of Portuno, the circular Temple of Hercules Victor and the Arch of Janus. Such direction would be taken again a century later by the city planning of the years 1928-1931.[5]

The transfer of the capital from Florence to Rome in 1870 was the occasion for the greatest transformations within the city. On July 5, the established date for the move, the city council faced the quandary of deciding how to resolve the many applications for residence in the new capital. Therefore, the council decided to place hundreds of families in twenty-six barns, re-utilized as apartments distributed on three floors, in via San Teodoro and via dei Fienili.[6] The Pantanella mills and pasta factories were placed behind Santa Maria in Cosmedin, in the same zone, still relatively marginal. In 1883, the Anglo-Roman society started the production of electric energy for public gas lighting in the vast depressed area of the Circus Maximus, sheltered from the view from the center.[7]

The city-planning of 1873 moved in the same direction towards the isolation of monuments required at the beginning of the century by the French. The new city-planning of 1883, with executive character, studied more detailed solutions

on the same indications of the previous plan: isolation of the Theater of Marcellus, connection of this zone with Piazza Bocca della Verità through the enlargement of the road in Via Bocca della Verità on the left side coming from the center. Similar decisions were programmed by the city-planning of 1909, but the demolition later realized would be much more extensive than originally planned.

The Commission for the layout of the Capitoline Hill, formed in 1919 under the direction of archaeologist Rodolfo Lanciani, along with, among others, architects A. Muñoz, G. Giovannoni, and P. Piacentini, was fundamental to the subsequent configuration of that area. Its line was the demolition of all the constructions set against the hill in order to expose the natural aspect of the tufaceous rock.

Also, the variations to the city planning of 1925 and 1926 tended toward demolition, and the areas to clear around San Nicola in Carcere were enlarged. In 1925, Antonio Muñoz, Commissioner for Lazio and Director of Antiquity and Fine Arts of the Governorship, directed the work beginning with the area close to the Arch of Janus for the isolation of the Temple of Portuno and the Temple of Hercules Victor. In 1926, the Theater of Marcellus was isolated; in 1928, the constructions on the slopes of the Capitol between Piazza dell'Ara Coeli and the Theater of Marcellus were demolished; and in 1931, the constructions around

San Nicola in Carcere were eliminated.

The city planning of 1931, with the choice of developing the city towards the sea, had a greater influence on this zone than other urban instruments. The Via del Mare began ideally right from the center, and the enlargement of Via Bocca della Verità was extended to both sides of the old road, creating in this way a perspective flight that, beyond the Theater of Marcellus, had the bell tower of Santa Maria in Cosmedin as its terminal pole. In 1932, the first tract of the Via del Mare was opened by Mussolini with the current Via dei Fori Imperiali for the tenth anniversary of the *March on Rome*. However, the demolition continued after 1936 to create space for the modern buildings

FIG. 4. *Extract of the Gregorian urban Cadaster (1818).*

of the city council that, aligned with the church of San Nicola in Carcere on one side and with the Casina of the Pierleoni on the other, almost reached the same height of the bell tower and the tower of those two monuments that in the re-planning of the area represented a sort of propylaea to the curving rise of Via del Mare towards Piazza Venezia. The new buildings, in brick and travertine and remarkable in size, were conceived in the programs of the Italian rationalist architecture as two continuous symmetric wings, opposed to the rarefaction of the green areas created around the isolated monuments, in an alternating system of full and empty spaces. Symmetrically at the sides of the road were the Theater of Marcellus and the Capitoline Hill, the green area around San Nicola in Carcere and that around the Casina of the Pierleoni, the compact mass of the two municipal building, and once again the green area around the monuments in the wide space of the *Foro Boario*. The necessity of this rhythmic condition of symmetry at the sides of the road also provided for the demolition of the church of Sant'Omobono, but the discovery of the sacred area between the church and the road determined the changes to the original project. In the final layout, the two buildings incorporated

the surviving monumental elements: the church of Sant'Omobono with its sacred area on the left side coming from Piazza Venezia, and the rich medieval residence of the Crescenzi, in the terminal part of the building of the registry office. Another house of the Pierleoni, previously placed in the area of this last building, was taken apart and rebuilt on the opposite side of the road, in correspondence with the Arch of Janus.[8] (Fig.4)

Street furniture, such as retaining walls, terracing, gardens, and travertine columns, played a fundamental role in the complex attempt to reconnect the isolated elements; and designed in an homogenous typology the new spaces created between the monuments, starting from the area of Monte Savello arriving at the slopes of the Capitol where the isolation of the hill and the exposure of the bare rock modified through the centuries by the insertion of constructions and even used as a quarry, assumed a symbolic character. The operation carried on by Muñoz required the realization of works of containment with spurs and terraces obtained from the retaining walls; a Latin vegetation composed of ilexes, cypresses, bay-trees and cluster pines was utilized in the attempt to give to the historical hill a more natural appearance and screen at the same time the artificial realizations.[9]

While the history of San Nicola in Carcere was strongly influenced by the urban context in which the church was placed, the case of Sant'Agnese fuori le Mura is completely different.

The complex (337-350 A.D.) formed by the church, the underground cemetery and the remains of a basilica erected by Emperor Constantine—or by his daughter Constantia who would also have her tomb built nearby (the Mausoleum of Constantia)—is located on Via Nomentana, an old road that started in a straight line from the Quirinale hill and led to *Nomentum* (Mentana). The old consular road,

FIG. 5. *Photos of the demolition work for the opening of the Via del Mare (ca. 1930).*

originally lined with villas, tombs, and graveyards, is in its current layout strongly characterized by late nineteenth century buildings. In fact, after Italian unification and the proclamation of Rome as the capital city, the government, and in particular Quintino Sella, strongly supported the choice to concentrate all the offices of the Ministries along Via Nomentana, in order to establish the new administrative axis of the Capital that, beginning from the Quirinale, the residence of the king, was at the same time close to Termini Station and to the new residential zones.

The program was partially realized, and the Ministries that were lined up along this road determined the severe tone of the palaces that represented the new housebuilding that developed along Via Nomentana with great alterations to a number of residential villas and gardens.[10]

The losses caused by the new constructions were relatively few: as for the ancient remains, it is worth mentioning the destruction of a necropolis in the spot where via Nomentana crosses the Aurelian Walls in correspondence with the large area occupied by the Ministry for Transportation.

Leaving Porta Pia and, past Villa Torlonia, continuing on the street on the left, one reaches Sant'Agnese (Fig 5). The whole complex is now completely inserted into the modern urban fabric and has lost any extra-urban connotation.

—Patrizio di Nezio

END NOTES

[1] P. Chini, "Il Foro Olitorio nell'antichità," in *La Casina dei Pierleoni*, Roma, 1999.
[2] The pilgrims who went to Rome in the Middle Ages to visit the places of cult, the relics of the Saints, and the ruins of the monuments, made use of the lists and desciptions of the itineraries, such as the "Mirabilia Urbis" and the "Itinerario of Einsiedeln." The graphic representations in this period were limited to representing architectonic and morphologic features in figurative and symbolic or pictorial terms.
[3] De Tournon was the head of the Commission for Embellishment, created to preserve ancient and modern monuments. The Commission also included Antonio Canova as the consultant for archaeological issues and Giuseppe Valdier as planner. With the arrival of Prefect De Tournon in Rome and the nomination of the Commission for Embellishment, a rationalization of the programs of intervention was realized, but again, almost all the works provided for gave priority to the aesthetic issues over all other aspects.
[4] We refer here to the transformations operated in Paris by Baron Haussmann between 1853 and 1870.
[5] G. Giovannoni, *Il programma edilizio del Prefetto di Roma conte De Tournon*, Nuova Antologia, Roma, 1927.
[6] I. Insolera, *Roma moderna*, Torino, 1962.
[7] A. Campitelli, "Lo sviluppo industriale a Roma dal XIX al XX sec.," *Le città europee. Nuove città e vecchi luoghi di lavoro*, Faenza, 1989.
[8] R. Motta, "Progetti e interventi urbanistici del XIX e XX secolo," *La Casina dei Pierleoni*, Roma, 1999.
[9] A Muñoz, *L'isolamento del colle Capitolino*, Roma, 1943.
[10] It was the will of Sella to concentrate all the Ministries along Via Nomentana; however, they were casually distributed throughout the city. Those lined up along the axis were the Ministry of Finances, the Minsitry of War, the Ministry of Agriculture and Forests, the Ministry of Public Works, the Ministry of Transportation, the Ministry of Labour, and the Ministry of National Debt.

While standing in front of an exhibit of frescoes removed from Roman churches, the viewer must use imagination to visualize Rome of the Middle Ages. It can take a remarkable effort, because it is difficult to find a single monument in the modern city—a basilica, a church, a baptistery—that is still intact and authentically medieval. In Rome, perhaps more than in any other place or city, monuments have been considered precious artifacts of memory and testimony, significant in the religious and political life of the Church. As guardians of the recollections of the beginning of the Christian era, popes, cardinals, and ambitious clients have considered it a due act of homage and prestige to restore, embellish, and decorate the great Roman "memories" of early Christian origin. However, renovating these monuments has often meant remaking them very radically, sometimes destroying them and completely rebuilding them. Therefore, although sites remain, architecture and their

FIG. 1. *Rome, Basilica of San Clemente: general view of the interior, showing the throne, the schola cantorum and the mosaic-apse. (photo ©Fototeca Nazionale, Ministero per i Beni Culturali e Ambientali)*

decorations change. No example is more meaningful than that of the patriarchal basilicas. San Giovanni in Laterano, San Peter's at the Vatican, and San Paolo Fuori le Mura are now Renaissance, baroque, nineteenth-century buildings with medieval roots that are difficult to recognize or that have been reduced to fragments. They possess none of the painted decorations that were seen and read by artists and clients throughout the Middle Ages as venerable prototypes and models to imitate.

It is even more important to remember that Roman pictorial art of the Middle Ages, now isolated from its context, reduced to fragments, to portable scenes that can travel from Italy to the United States like a Flemish painting or a Picasso drawing, was originally a product with a different vocation and an integral bond to the sacred building in which it originated. The integration of "figures" in the general layout of ecclesiastical space began early in the politics and taste of Christian and Papal Rome. Images, as representations of divinity or as a narration of sacred stories, soon became indispensable to the relationship between the Church and its believers. This is the great novelty of Christian art compared to that of antiquity. If the art of ancient and imperial Rome had been a public art, characterized by enormous constructions, gigantic epigraphic writing, wide-spread statuaries in the streets, squares, and forums, Christian art seems to privilege the interior of churches from the very beginning. It emphasized the importance of the zone of the apse and the altar with the brightest and most precious decoration— the mosaic (fig.1). Instead, the walls of the naves, which believers "read" on their way to the altar, were adorned with cycles of

FIG 2. *Rome, church of Santa Cecilia in Trastevere: Jacob's Dream, thirteenth century fresco by Pietro Cavallini (detail showing the cosmatesque work of the column, as reproduced in A.M. ROMANINI, Roma nel Duecento. L'arte nella città dei papi da Innocenzo III a Bonifacio VIII, Torino 1991, p. 375). (photo ©Fototeca Nazionale, Ministero per i Beni Culturali e Ambientali)*

since the first centuries of the Middle Ages and extremely venerated. However, this typology of sacred objects does not contradict what appears to be a general and founding characteristic of the mentality of the papal city, that is, an interest in the great value of sacred places and monuments. In Rome, in fact, icons were tied in an indivisible way to the monuments that housed them. A good example of this is the great portrait of Christ, of which remain only fragments today, but that was believed to be a portrait of the Savior, "authentic" and therefore miraculous and of supernatural origin. (The painting has always been in the Sancta Sanctorum chapel in the Lateran, probably built in the first centuries of the Christian era expressly to host the icon.) Other examples include the city's

sacred narration, almost always in the rapid, effective technique of the fresco. The choice of medium underwent few changes during the course of the Middle Ages: mosaics were very suitable in fixing the images of divine apparitions in the space of the apse—a metaphor for the mystical around and beyond the altar—while the narrative vocation reserved for the long surfaces of the naves gave rise to a ductile repertoire of the visual translation of sacred history largely based on the two opposing cycles of the Old and New Testament and on the stories of the saints

On the other hand, the Roman Middle Ages produced very few mobile paintings. To understand this, one must remember that in the churches of the city, mass was recited facing the believers, *versus populum*; the priest, therefore, stood behind the altar, with his back to the apse. Thus, an altar piece or polypthyc would have represented an obstacle between he who said the mass and his audience. The only "mobile" pieces in Rome were the icons, a genre documented in the city

churches dedicated to the Virgin: each one had its own image of Mary, always very old, whose origin was lost in legend. In the great icon of the church of Santa Maria in Trastevere (fig. 2), in front of the image of the Virgin, the pontiff who commissioned the icon is portrayed on his knees venerating the Virgin. It is in this way that the veneration paid to Mary and the almost personal relationship between the "humble" pope and the Virgin queen is fixed in a figure.

It is therefore wrong, or anachronistic, to think of Roman medieval painting simply as a decorative instrument. At least in the most important and organic cases, it probably had a didactic and political function equal or superior to that of sacred literature—superior because it was a much more popular instrument, visible to a very large number of people who, if they could not read, could certainly look at the painted characters and stories. Figures then could be a real "text" expressed in very special, engaging language, whose emotional and intellectual impact is hard for us to measure. In a world that knew far fewer images than the world we know today, those images acquired a tremendous significance, and sometimes were seen as almost miraculous, of a nature suspended between divine and human, between the direct manifestation of divinity and the terms in which divinity Himself was humanly represented.

The stakes then were remarkable, and this became the way in which the work of the artist came into direct contact with the most important groups of power of the city—and certainly not only those of Rome—including the pontiff, the cardinals, and the great religious orders, among which the Benedictines stood out throughout the Middle Ages. These powerful leaders became the interlocutors of the

FIG. 3. *Rome, Basilica of San Clemente (lower level): fresco in the narthex showing A Miracle at the Tomb of St. Clemente. (photo ©Fototeca Nazionale, Ministero per i Beni Culturali e Ambientali)*

contributed to clothe the interior of churches and combined with the other media. It is enough to look at one of the best preserved interiors that remains today, the upper basilica of San Clemente, where the sculpted marbles, the enclosure of the choir of the monks, and the throne reserved for the pontiff fit into the liturgical space dominated by the great mosaic of the apse that portrays the Cross between *girali*—leaves of acanthus in the form of a spiral with a flower in the center—a clear symbol of the Church living out of the sacrifice of Christ (fig. 3).

The production of liturgical ornaments in Rome was dominated for centuries, at least from the eleventh to the fourteenth and even fifteenth

artists, those who commissioned and controlled their work, who paid and protected them. Clients and artists were constantly engaged in a race for excellency and were rivals in prestige and ostentation.

In light of this situation, the Roman workshops were forced to develop an articulate and efficient working system. The way the medieval artists worked was substantially different from the situations of artists to whom we automatically refer—the great artists of the Renaissance, who were at the same time courtiers and intellectuals, and whose personalities shone, individual and sometimes solitary; modern artists, even more, who manage themselves and the market of their art. These parameters do not help us to imagine the ways in which art was produced in medieval Rome. Instead, we can understand better if, for a moment, we move from the field of painting to that of liturgical ornaments and decorative sculpture. The production of pulpits, ambos, candelabra, pontifical thrones, and floorings, was clearly essential to religious functions and therefore to the needs of priests, monks, bishops, cardinals, and the pontiff himself. It was, in fact, a production that stood in a tight dialectic relationship with the pictorial decorations: liturgical ornaments

centuries, by the workshops of the Roman marble workers, the so-called Maestri Cosmateschi (derived from the name of one of the members, Cosma), by systems that we can define as monopolistic. Studies of both the past and present agree that these workshops were characterized by an organization based completely on family structures. The inscriptions with which these artists proudly signed their works specified the names of the authors—that is, of the heads of the workshops—accompanied by those of their sons; or at times, the signing artist identified himself as "son," thus designating himself the heir of the workshop of the father. It was a budding industry and certainly an highly organized craft. A panoramic look at the works left and signed by the marble workers in Rome and the surrounding region demonstrates the fact that each workshop was the exclusive contractor of a construction site; that is, a church and two workshops never coexisted in the same place at the same time.

In short, the competition was rigorous and the spaces to be conquered were occupied and defended with a determination that is reminiscent of more recent battles for the conquest of new markets. The situation of the workshops of the painters was probably similar; however, the first thing one notices — despite the scarcer documentation — is that, compared to that of the sculptors, the work of the painters remains largely anonymous, at least until the end of the thirteenth century when the names of individual and recognizable artists began to emerge, starting with Jacopo Torriti, an artist of the papal court, and Pietro Cavallini, a great painter who mainly worked for the city's religious orders and convents. Roman painters did not sign many of their works and did not leave their names on great proud inscriptions as the marble workers did. Even taking into account the serious destruction the Roman medieval artistic patrimony underwent, the absence of painters' names is a stark reality, confirmed by the silence of the more extensive sixteenth and seventeenth-century documentation that, with its rich descriptions and drawings, has preserved the memory of the great medieval monuments and filled in some gaps on what has been lost.

There are, however, a few exceptions. In the eleventh century, we know the names of two painters who signed the icon of Sant'Angelo in Pescheria: "Petrus de Belizo" and "Bellushomo." It is impossible to separate the execution of the painting between two "hands"—unfortunately, the icon has been stolen and remains lost—and the double signature could be more a trademark of the workshop than an autographic division. Not many years later, in the basilica of Sant'Anastasio in Castel Sant'Elia near Nepi, in the surroundings of Rome, a great cycle of frescoes with an apocalyptic and hagiographic theme was realized. In the apse, right below the

FIG.4. *Rome, Sancta Sanctorum Chapel: the Acheropita. (photo © Vatican Museums, Photographic Archives.)*

great theophany, we have evidence that the workshop of the painters active in that site had a family structure: the inscription, in fact, attributes the paternity of the work to "Iohannes et Stefanus fratres pictores romani" and to their nephew Iohannes. It is difficult to ascertain whether the first two were brothers, or whether they were monks instead, but the qualification of "nepos" attributed to the third is unquestionable. Later, at the end of the thirteenth century, a father and a son, Paolo and Filippo, signed the frescoes on the portico of San Lorenzo fuori le Mura. Almost in the same years, finally, we know that the basilica of Sant'Agnese fuori le Mura hosted a great complex of frescoes that were completed with long inscriptions of the names of the painters - "Nicolaus V," "Johannes VI," "Johannes VII," and "Johannes XXI" (the numeral posted next to the name seems to indicate family and occupational dynasties). These inscriptions did not survive. However, at least a part of the frescoes of Sant'Agnese has reached us, detached in the nineteenth century, now safe in the Pinacoteca Vaticana and displayed in this exhibit. The stories of Saint Catherine, the Marriage of the Virgin, and the other fragments that are now well-known are works of the late thirteenth century, magnificent examples of Roman painting in the time of Giotto. Instead, other fragments are clearly older works, probably from the end of the twelfth or the beginning of the thirteenth century, and help us to imagine the medieval basilica, heavily decorated, colored, historiated by later trends and different times. They attest to the constant preoccupation of clients and painters to tell stories on the walls of sacred buildings.

Let us return for a moment to the workshops of the marble workers—in fact, they possessed a characteristic that is invaluable in understanding something in the distant field of painting. The marble workers were, among the Roman artists, those who had a more intimate bond with the past of the city of Rome, that is the ancient city. They were authorized to pick through the ancient monuments for pieces they could use: they recycled marbles, capitals, columns, reused them in their entirety or in sections. With these spoils, they created new works that did not have anything to do with the ancient aesthetic, but were made from the same materials. Painters, certainly, could not do the same thing: drawing among the ancient frescoes—which must have existed in large number in medieval Rome—was not as easy. Even without considering the problem of the non-Christian iconographic content of the ancient pagan paintings, recycling them was evidently impossible.

The memory of ancient painting happened to survive and to become more evident in the workshops of the Roman painters in a more roundabout manner. Ancient decorative repertoires and the deceptive make-up of the walls particularly struck the fantasy of medieval masters: single elements and motifs—friezes, Greek keys, fish, birds, brackets, flowers, bunches of grapes—shared the repertoires of ancient painting and ancient Christian painting from the catacombs. The more ambitious pictorial systems intended to suggest a simulated space: columns and architraves in perspective, foreshortened brackets, painted optical illusions (trompe l'oeil) or fake stucco mixed into the pictorial background.

Roman masters must have considered this ancient visual and pictorial patrimony as a real reserve of patterns to be incorporated as their own professional "tools." They periodically emerged and periodically disappeared whenever the abstract and geometric mentality that represented the other wing of medieval thinking became predominant. We do not know if painters, from

FIG. 5. *Rome, Basilica of San Clemente (lower level): detail of the decoration underneath the fresco cycle with Stories of St. Alessius. (photo ©Fototeca Nazionale, Ministero per i Beni Culturali e Ambientali)*

time to time, would find inspiration from those monuments that represented the prototypes of late ancient and medieval painting; for example, we cannot ascertain whether medieval masters considered the early Christian frescoes in the naves of Saint Peter's or San Paolo as real models—texts to study. However, we have good reason to believe that such was the case, as we realize that the lost cycles of Saint Peter's and San Paolo, as they are recorded by seventeenth and eighteenth-century sources and drawings, had long series of stories on the walls of the central nave, framed in a system of deceptive architecture of architraves and columns, perhaps stucco, perhaps painted, that determined an impression of the relief. The same solution, this time clearly painted, returns at the end of the thirteenth century in the cycle of stories from the Old Testament created by Pietro Cavallini in Santa Cecilia in Trastevere: the "loan" is certainly not accidental. Cavallini organized the nave of Santa Cecilia with opposing stories of the Old and New Testament, in much the way they were depicted in the early Christian Basilicas and as he could still witness in Saint Peter's in the Vatican (fig.4).

We can argue therefore that, for this point, there is an alternating continuity between the ancient and late ancient experience and the pictorial culture of the medieval masters. Another motif borrowed from antiquity periodically emerges in the work of the Roman painters, and examples of this appear in this exhibit in some of the frescoed fragments. I am referring to the frescoes detached from the crypt of San Nicola in Carcere, an important monument that was decorated around the 1120s or 1130s. It was probably a rather narrow space, covered with a series of small vaults that offered triangular spaces to the painter's brush or, at the top of the walls, small lunettes. We can see them today, even though they have been removed from their original system: the paintings are marked by a very decorative and elegant taste, and their surfaces are covered with friezes and elements of that same repertoire that was, as we have already mentioned, part of an ancient legacy shared by the paintings of the catacombs: birds, baskets of fruits and flowers, fishes, female heads as masks, and so on. Other important churches were painted in the same years with a different syntax, but with similar motifs: for example, the structure of the lower basilica of San Clemente was reinforced around the end of the eleventh century with pillars that were immediately frescoed with *Stories of Saint Clement and Other Saints* (fig. 5). Another example is the nave of Santa Maria in Cosmedin where a great cycle of stories from the Old Testament, with the life and deeds of the prophets Daniel and Ezekiel, was realized at the beginning of the twelfth century (fig.6). The scenes of this cycle are not free on the wall but are framed by a great painted architecture, with columns and architraves, decorative masks, cloths thrown on the architraves, shells, cornucopias: in short, once again the idea of deceptive

Above: FIG. 6. *Rome, church of Santa Maria in Cosmedin: remains of the twelfth century fresco decorating the central nave. (photo ©Fototeca Nazionale, Ministero per i Beni Culturali e Ambientali)*

architecture that was present in the basilicas of Saint Peter's and San Paolo appears, and cannot but evoke a late ancient taste.

It has been proposed often, and with good reason, that this trend after the ancient fashion that predominated between the eleventh and twelfth centuries in the decoration of Roman churches, represented the artistic "side" of the broader program of the Roman church that was emerging from a serious crisis of moral decadence and struggle with the Empire, and that had to recreate and restore its virginity. To achieve that goal, it appealed to the beginning of its history, to the heroic times, to the early Christian era (fig. 7). The monuments that apparently drew new interest and inspired emulation dated back to that same period. It is difficult to know for certain if that was actually the case: visual and artistic phenomena are always, to a certain degree, unfathomable, and artistic creation always eludes the attempts to frame it too tightly within political intentions and the propaganda of a regime. However, the

Far Left: FIG. 7. *Rome, church of Santa Maria in Trastevere: the Madonna della Clemenza.(photo ©Fototeca Nazionale, Ministero per i Beni Culturali e Ambientali)*
Left: FIG.8. *Rome, church of Sant'Angelo in Pescheria (formerly): Icon of the Virgin with Child. (photo ©Fototeca Nazionale, Ministero per i Beni Culturali e Ambientali)*

fact that Roman sacred buildings have always been the object of true decorative trends, especially during periods in which the Church and its representatives had a particular need to use the visual and artistic medium as a supplementary instrument in their operations, convinces us to attribute to art, and in this case to pictorial art of the Roman Middle Ages, not only an extraordinary aesthetic value and symbolic force, but also a primary role in the whole political and spiritual history of the Middle Ages.

—Serena Romano

ENDNOTES

[1] Charles de Brosses, president for life of the Parliament of Bourgoigne (Digione 1709-Paris 1777), was a versatile scholar of history, archeology, geography, and linguistics.

[2] C. de Brosses, *Viaggio in Italia*, Rome, 1973, Letter XLVIII, p. 481.

[3] The tradition of *stacco a massello* can already be found in the time of classical antiquity. Pliny and Vitruvius narrate, in fact, how fragments of the mural painting of Sparta was transferred to Rome (*Naturalis Historia* libro XXXV and *De architectura* libro II). News of this practice can also be found during the Renaissance when the operation of cutting the walls was habitually entrusted to a sculptor whose technical abilities would prevent inopportune fracturing of the artwork.

[4] "...how they could remove the fresco paintings from the wall, detaching the wall behind without damaging the picture. After having literally broken the wall along all its length, they fixed some beams on one side as a frame and the same thing is done on the other side as well as along the top. When everything is stable, fixed, and pressed with iron levers, it is lifted in order to be able to cut the bottom and apply the fourth corner of the frame. Then, it is all removed and transferred using machines." C. de Brosses, *Viaggio*, cit., Lettera XLVIII, p. 481.

[5] Even Michelangelo did not hesitate to destroy the frescoes by Perugino on the wall of the altar of the Sistine Chapel in order to paint his *Last Judgement*.

[6] In turn, the same *Last Judgement* risked being destroyed in 1564 when the order came to remove all those paintings in the churches that contained obscene images or images which did not conform to the regulations of the Council of Trent.

[7] The thirteen visages of *Angels* and *Apostles* are conserved in the Pinacoteca Vaticana, and the *Redemptor* is at the Palazzo del Quirinale.

[8] "...Taja, describing them in the chapter house of Saint Peter's, specifies that they were saved due also to his intervention and that of Father Sebastiano Resta, the noted collector of drawings." A. Conti in *Storia del Restauro e della conservazione delle opere d'arte*, Milano 1973, cap.V, p. 118.

[9] C. de Brosses, *Viaggio* cit., Lettera XLVIII, p. 482.

[10] In some cases, sacred images considered miraculous were moved from the places they were found and placed in the centers of new churches dedicated to them.

[11] Approximately 25 years ago, Federico Zeri, called "Forger in Calcinaccio," the author of a series of forgeries in plaster. In 1994, G. Mazzoni definitively identified him as the forger from Siena, Umberto Giunti (1886-1970).

[12] It is the case of the Etruscan frescoes of the Tomb of Francois di Vulci that were removed in 1863 due to high humidity and the formation of concretions on the surface of the painting, and were subjected to further intervention by transferring them to hempen cloth in 1947. In 1987, certain fragments preserved at the Villa Albani in Rome were definitively mounted on panels of Aerolam (a *sandwich* constituted of nests of bees between two layers of glass wool and polyester resin and hardened by an anodized aluminum structure) and restored, under my supervision, at the Laboratorio di Restauro dei Musei Vaticani on the occasion of the exhibit for the 150th anniversary of the Museo Gregoriano Etrusco.

[13] Cesare Brandi (Siena 1906-Vignano 1988) was an art critic and founder of the Istituto Centrale del Restauro.

[14] The word derives from the term "Sinopis," a red earth with a base of oxidized iron, already known by the Romans and the Greeks and coming from the ancient city of Sinope on the Black Sea. The color was used to trace the first sketch of the composition on *arriccio*, that is, on that plaster layer that came in direct contact with the wall upon which was applied the plaster for the application of the fresco pigments.

[15] Other terms of the animal *colla forte*: *colla cervione*, *colla di Zurigo*, *colla da falegname*.

[16] Molasses is a dense, brown , sweet liquid that is the residue of the refinement of sugar.

[17] Term commonly used at the time to describe a restorer specialized in "extractions" (*stacchi* and *strappi*) of mural paintings.

[18] *Scialbo* is the covering layer (commonly of lime) applied in the course of the centuries on the paintings generally for hygenic motives after the plague.

[19] Cadorite is an expanded material that has been used at the Laboratorio Restauro Dipinti dei Musei Vaticani since the end of the 1960s.

[20] The intervention has been executed by restorer Fabio Piacentini of the Laboratorio Restauro Pitture dei Musei Vaticani who served as director for the work group composed by F. Prantera with the collaboration of F. Leopardini, a contract worker, and restorers F. Cantisani, B. Marocchini, and S. Zucconi who served as external collaborators in charge of the restoration, following the directions provided, on five of the fragments: inv. 40476, 40481, 40485, 40494, 40516.

The supports for the paintings have been constructed by M. Alesi and M. Mattarocci of the Laboratio Restauro Manufatti Lignei dei Musei Vaticani; the photographic documentation has been executed by F. Bono, A. Bracchetti, L. Giordano, D. Pivato, and P. Zigrossi of the Laboratorio Fotografico dei Musei Vaticani. The system of suspension of the paintings has been overseen by the firm F. De Simone, Rome.

REFERENCES

Guglielmo Matthiae, *Pittura romana del Medioevo,* Roma, 1966 (aggiornamento scientifico a cura di Maria Andaloro e Francesco Gandolfo, Roma, 1987-1988)

Guglielmo Matthiae, *Mosaici medievali delle chiese di Roma, Roma,* 1967

Helène Toubert, *Le renouveau paléochrétien à Rome au début du XII siècle*, Cahiers Archéologiques, 29 (1970), 99-154 (rist. in Helène Toubert, Un art dirigé, Parigi, 1990)

Peter Cornelius Claussen, *Magistri Doctissimi Romani. Die Römische Marmorkünstler des Mittelalters* (Corpus Cosmatorum I), Wiesbaden, 1987

Maria Andaloro, Alessandra Ghidoli, Antonio Iacobini, Serena Romano, Alessandro Tomei ed., Fragmenta Picta, catalogo della mostra, Roma, 1989

Herbert Kessler, "Caput et mater omnium ecclesiarum: Old St.Peter's Church Decoration in Medieval Latium," in *Italian Church Decoration of the Middle Ages and Early Renaissance*, ed. William Tronzo, (atti delle giornate di studio, Frenze, Villa Spelman, 1987), Bologna-Baltimore, 1989, 119-146

Enrico Parlato, Serena Romano, Roma e il Lazio, Milano, 1992

Sancta Sanctorum, Milano, 1995

Maria Andaloro, Serena Romano, Arte e iconografia a Roma da Costantino a Cola di Rienzo, Milano, 2000

THE FRESCOES OF SANT'AGNESE FUORI LE MURA

Outside the city walls of ancient Rome, on the *Via Nomentana,* one of the main thoroughfares to and from the northeast, lies the church of *Sant'Agnese fuori le Mura* (St. Agnes Outside the Walls). Since the burial of the dead was not allowed within the city in ancient times, tombs were located along the major traffic arteries. It was either a daughter or a niece of Emperor Constantine the Great (A.D. 306–337), by the name of Constanza, who in A.D. 342 officially established the Christian cult at this site by building a massive cemetery basilica over the catacomb on the *Via Nomentana,* in which the virgin martyr Agnes is venerated. Next to this church she then chose the place for her own mausoleum. She was buried there in a porphyry (dark red stone) sarcophagus which is now in the Vatican museum. This centralized building was later used as a baptistry, and then in A.D. 1254 it was consecrated as a church dedicated to St. Constanza. With its rich mosaic decoration it is one of the most spectacular and outstanding monuments from the early Christian period in Rome which preserves its original character almost completely.

The fourth century cemetery basilica with its enormous dimensions was already in ruins by the seventh century. Therefore Pope Honorius (A.D. 625–638) built a much smaller church facing the original site, but still immediately above the grave of the martyr. Since the new building cuts into the steeply sloping terrain and should be accessible from both levels, it required a special architectural form. A Byzantine style balcony church was chosen to make it possible for people to enter either from the level of the original church or from the higher level of the *Via Nomentana.* Interior balconies run around three sides and are connected by staircases to the ground floor where the altar is located in an apse which soars to enclose both levels. Other examples of this architectural form in Rome can be seen in the early Christian basilicas of *San Lorenzo fuori le Mura* and in the church of St. Nereus and St. Achilleus in the *Via Appia.*

The Benedictine nuns, who in the course of the Middle Ages had established their convent in St. Agnes, made use of this special arrangement of the spaces and developed the concept for the decoration and the paintings accordingly. Indeed the seventeenth century *Commentary on the Basilica of St. Agnes, Gallicanus, and Costantin on the Nomentana Way (Commentarius de Basilica S. Agnetis, Gallicani et Costantini in Via Nomentana)* by Martinus Milesius Sarazanius (commonly known as Marzio Milesi) primarily describes large fresco cycles on the walls of the upper left gallery. It is essentially to these that the fragments belong which are displayed in the exhibition.

In the following centuries these wall paintings were covered with whitewash and forgotten. Pope Pius IX had a distinct reverence for this site, especially after he experienced the spectacular collapse of the ceiling of an assembly room in the *canonica* on the 12th of April 1855, when he found himself all of a sudden quite unexpectedly in the basement of the building. All of that led to his funding of a complete renovation of the church rooms of the seventh century basilica. In the course of this effort the fresco fragments on display here were discovered along with others which are now in the Vatican Museum. Pellegrino Succi used the *Stacco—technique* to extract the frescoes from the wall, i.e. they were taken off along with part of the substance of the wall on which they are painted, and he transferred them to canvas backing. When the inventory was done, apparently no attention was paid to the order of the narrative scenes depicted. Morever for a long time their precise orignal location within the church was unknown. Only in recent years has the text by Milesi been studied anew in order to interpret the frescoes, and their original context has been rediscovered. Two apparently complete cycles and elements of other pictorial sequences emerged as a result of the events of 1855. One of the cycles illustrates the life of St. Catherine and the other one depicts the life of the founder of the Order, St Benedict. The iconography of a third set, of which only two scenes have been preserved, has not yet been identified.

The Catherine cycle is more or less faithful to the description of the saint as related in the *Legende Aurea*, a collection of legends from the Middle Ages arranged by Jacopo da Voragine and commonly used in that time period by painters as a source for their illustrations. Since eleven scenes from the Catherine cycle have been either completely or at least partially preserved, as well as eleven from the Benedict cycle, it may be assumed that both cycles are complete. Fragments which cannot be assigned indicate paintings outside these two sequences.

Two more scenes (inv. 40494 and 40519) were executed by the same workshop as the Catherine legend, but they indicate the existence of a third cycle.

Stylistically the Catherine cycle and the two additional frescoes are seen as following in the line of the "Last Judgement" in the Church of St. Cecilia in Trastevere, painted in A.D. 1293 by Pietro Cavallini, and in close relation to the frescoes depicting the Archdeacons Stephanus and Laurentius in the entryway to the previously mentioned *San Lorenzo fuori le Mura*. The approximate date of the cycle is assigned to the Pontificate of Boniface VIII (A.D. 1294–1303). Milesi also recorded the signatures or inscriptions with the names of various painters; evidently reflecting the members, or perhaps generations, of a family when they designate themselves as Nicholas V, John VI, John VIII, or John XXI. The names themselves, however, cannot be correlated with any known artists. Rather they confirm the differences in the manner of painting which can be noticed among the separate wall sections when compared with each other. One can assume that a large workshop was at work here as is common in such undertakings. The crew does not seem, however, to have been very homogeneous in their manner of painting, nor to have been directed by a principal artist; rather each individual painter could allow his own style to unfold.

The Benedict cycle, whose scenes are more fragmentary than the ones from the life of St. Catherine, is completely autonomous. Even just the ornamentation of the frames, which is slightly illusion, makes it very clear that it is artistically independent of the Catherine cycle. Since they both come from the same gallery level in the church, they have shared the same fate, even to their manner of preservation through the *Stacco—technique* and in the research that has been done to study them. The iconography of the Benedict cycle is also oriented toward the *Legenda Aurea* or a related text which was derived from the *Dialoghi* by Gregory the Great.

Based on the stronger influence of Giotto, the style of the Benedict cycle should be dated somewhat later than the Catherine cycle and is attributed to the painter Lello da Orvieto. In the oeuvre the frescos would fit in the years between A.D. 1322–25 and 1340, a period in which it is surmised that he was active in Rome.

As is evident from the overpainting of parts in the Benedict cycle with single figures of other saints (inv. 40477) and from the stylistic differences (inv. 40485 and 40586), a second phase of painting followed closely after completion of this cycle. The attribution to various artists and workshops (workshop of the Catherine legend, Lello da Orvieto, painters of the second phase, as well as probably further painters of additional figures of saints), the varying typology (scenes alternate with the single figures, the latter again distinguished between those painted within an architectural setting and others in front of decorative backgrounds), the independent iconographies among the cycles (three distinct, separate cycles and figures of saints as well as single figures within an architectural as in compositional setting), and the varying styles (on the one hand of the Catherine legend and the Benedict cycle and on to the other hand of the overpaintings and the second phase of the paintings) do not at all indicate that the murals from *St Agnese fuori le Mura* come from an originally homogeneous decorative system. The preserved fragments denote an originally complex situation out of which the initial setting has to be reconstructed. The changes which were made over the course of the years also indicate that the Benedictine nuns cultivated a lively interaction with their church.

After the murals in the chapel *Sancta Sanctorum* at the *Lateran,* the cycles and frescoes of St. Agnes are the best preserved wall paintings of the late middle ages in Rome. They are an example of artistic activity under Boniface VIII, who in A.D. 1300 proclaimed the first Holy Year. The commissions for the many paintings, however, seem to have come less from the Pope himself.

When the first *Stacchi* were mounted by Pellegrino Succi, the size of the frames over which the canvas was stretched was determined by the sections of the wall from which the murals were being detached. Only in cases in which a fragment was preserved without its context were such remnants mounted in that way on their new stretcher. While in an earlier restoration of some of the frescoes only the perserved original substance was considered and the sizes of the frames was reduced, in the current campaign attention is paid again to their relation amongst each other: the height of all panels is uniform, but guided by their painted ornamental frames, the frescoes are positioned and oriented on their stretchers so the original horizontal relationships of the single scenes are reconstructed. In order to achieve the same result for the vertical relationship, more information about the framework would be required. Unfortunately none of that has been preserved or handed down. Remnants for which no point of reference for their original context survived must simply be accepted in their fragmentary character.

—Arnold Nesselrath

FRESCOES FROM THE WORKSHOP OF THE CATHERINE MASTERS

The Catherine Legend

Workshop of the Catherine Legend
St. Catherine Asks God for Enlightenment before the Disputation with the Lawyers

Detached Fresco (Stacco); Fragment
140 x 159 cm (Fragment)
151 x 160 cm (Stretcher)
Vatican Museums, inv. 40470

The scene is the second episode represented in the cycle. The composition is symmetrically arranged, nevertheless all elements draw attention to the figure of St. Catherine. In the center the powerful Emperor sits enthroned and summons his lawyers to debate with Catherine. Although he turns to them he points to the kneeling saint, toward whom the throne is oriented. Catherine urgently appeals to the angel above her. Despite her pose she is almost as large as the soldiers behind her and her opponents, the lawyers. By virtue of their proportions, Catherine and the Emperor are both the main characters and the opposing poles in the scene.

At the bottom left border only the word "Ubi," the beginning of the titulus is preserved.

Workshop of the Catherine Legend

St. Catherine Debates with the Lawyers of Emperor Maxentius

Detached Fresco (Stacco); Fragment
157 x 153 cm (Fragment)
165 x 157 cm (Stretcher)
Vatican Museums, inv. 40516

This scene follows immediately after the previous one. Again St. Catherine and the Emperor are the antipodes, but they stand opposite one another at the edges of the picture. The sitting Emperor is the same height as the standing lawyers, who fill the picture past the center. Catherine, who stands at the left edge, is larger than all others. She dominates the scene with her rhetorical gesture and draws all attention to herself.

   At the bottom of the picture area the titulus is mostly preserved; the missing letters can easily be filled in: "Ubi disputavit cum philosophis. Massentius Imperator:"

Workshop of the Catherine Legend

THE SCOURGING OF
ST. CATHERINE

Detached Fresco (Stacco); Fragment
155 x 154 cm (Fragment);
165 x 160 cm (Stretcher)
Vatican Museums, inv. 40476

Each of the two opposing figures,
Emperor Maxentius and St.
Catherine, dominated one-half of
the picture area before the fresco
was heavily damaged. The figure of
the ruler was larger; however the
composition was balanced by the
facts that the female figure is
viewed frontally and that the
two much smaller servants
wielding the scourges are arranged
symmetrically to her. Seen half
naked from the front and with
the palms of her hands turned
outward, Catherine not only suffers
the same torment as Christ, but her
imitatio is also formally expressed in
her Christ-like figure.

Under the picture area this title is
also mostly preserved; the missing
letters can easily be filled in:
"Maxentius Imperator: Ubi fuit
verberata." The two-part
composition, that is, the opposing
positions of the protagonists,
is emphasized by the title of
the picture.

Workshop of the Catherine Legend

The Dead Bodies of the Converted and Burned Lawyers are Collected by the Christians and Buried

Detached Fresco (Stacco); Fragment
148 x 155.5 cm (Fragment)
165 x 160 cm (Strecher)
Vatican Museums, inv. 40481

This scene is not common in all of the Catherine cycles; it does not always appear and demonstrates the comprehensive character of the cycle from Sant'Agnese fuori le Mura as well as the extent of the area available in this basilica. The seven lawyers can be seen in the center with closed eyes in the midst of the flames. To the left are four, and to the right three assistants who interact with the martyrs.

In the center of the upper picture area, remnants of an inscription can be made out. However, it is no longer legible.

PERFILIVS   ACVSFA IPATRIS

✝ VBI VISITATA E ABAGVS

Workshop of the Catherine Legend

CATHERINE IN PRISON
CONVERTS THE
EMPRESS FAUSTINA AND
GENERAL PORPHYRIUS

Detached Fresco (Stacco); Fragment
158 x 152 cm (Fragment)
165 x 154.5 cm (Stretcher)
Vatican Museums, inv. 40467

The entire upper left quarter of the
fresco was almost completely
destroyed. But since the titulus is
preserved the iconography scene
can be positively identified. Below
the picture one reads: "Perfilius,"
"Augusta Imperatris," and "Ubi
visitata est ab Augusta."

The image is divided into two
parts. The left half is nearly filled
by the two converts, General
Porphyrius and Empress Faustina.
The prison bars and the dark
background mark the compositional contrast to the saint. Her
raised right hand indicates that she
is in dialog with the two visitors.

Workshop of the Catherine Legend

CATHERINE IS TORTURED ON THE WHEEL, BUT THE MARTYR WHEELS ARE DESTROYED

Detached Fresco (Stacco); Fragment
157 x 152 cm (Fragment)
165 x 156.5 cm (Stretcher)
Vatican Museums, inv. 40478

The salvation of St. Catherine from the martyrdom intended for her of being broken on the wheel has often been depicted. It is from this episode that one of her attributes is derived, with which she is most often pictured, the wheel. The various actions represented in the mural have obviously prevented a clearly organized composition like most of the other frescos in this cycle. Nearly two-thirds of the area of the picture is taken up by the famous *martyrium*. While the idealized saint, covered only with a loincloth and identified by a crown, is saved by an angel, the eager spectators are seen cowering in the background on the right; and in the foreground an executioner comes under the wheels himself. The left part of the picture is filled out with the imperial pair in discussion with one another. The Empress solicits mercy for Catherine from her husband. The ruler indicates his embarrassment by placing his left hand on his chin, but stubbornly continues to watch the spectacle.

Workshop of the Catherine Legend

St. Catherine is Beheaded

Detached Fresco (Stacco); Fragment
70 x 139 cm (Fragment)
73.5 x 141 cm (Stretcher)
Vatican Museums, inv. 40480

The central part of the composition is taken up by the executioner who returns his sword to its sheath after having carried out the sentence decreed by the Emperor. On the left the ruler himself sits majestically in the judgment arbour and watches the execution. On the right the headless body of St. Catherine is falling forward. The waving cloak of the executioner as background for his piercing gaze heightens the dramatic effect of the episode.

This fresco is perhaps the most famous of the whole series.

Two Scenes of an unidentified cycle in addition to the Catherine Legend

Workshop of the Catherine Legend

Scene from the Life of a Saint

Detached Fresco (Stacco); Fragment
53.5 x 104 cm (Fragment)
55.5 x 107.5 cm (Stretcher)
Vatican Museums inv. 40519

The place of these figures within the entire original composition cannot be determined, since no point of reference for the frame of the scene is preserved. Considering that the protagonist is wearing a veil, just as are her two attendants, it cannot be a representation from the life of the princess, St. Catherine. A comparison of the types of the heads, the way of applying colors, the modeling of the volumes, the contouring, or the heightening of lights leaves no doubt that this fresco, along with a second fragment of an unidentified scene (inv. 40494) has to be attributed to the painters of this cycle and not of the Benedict cycle. Its iconography fits in with neither one; the male figure on the right is certainly not St. Benedict. The hypothesis that it could be a part of "The Marriage of Mary" is contradicted by the preponderance of veiled saints and the missing halo of the approaching male figure, who cannot then be Joseph. Volbach's interpretation as "History of a holy Nun" is appealing for various reasons. Milesi's descriptions from the seventeenth century mentions paintings besides the two cycles, and also the paintings under the roof still have to be interpreted and their context has to be analyzed. This fragment is one of the best produced by this workshop.

Workshop of the Catherine Legend

Scene from the Life of a Saint

Detached Fresco (Stacco); Fragment
128 x 118 cm (Fragment)
161 x 126 cm (Stretcher)
Vatican Museums, inv. 40494

Like the previous fragment, this scene cannot be explained in conjunction with the Catherine legend. However the style of painting, especially the facial types, are so close to those depicted in the life of this saint, that this mural can also be attributed to this workshop.

Portrayed is a bearded male saint not unlike the man without a halo in the previous scene (inv. 40519). He holds a short staff and is looking at a person who stood before a spiral column, but because of the heavy damage to this fresco only the raised hands are preserved. The saint is accompanied by five figures, at least three of them female, who also carry short staves and support him in his endeavor.

Lello da Orvieto

St. Benedict Receives a Visit on Easter Sunday from a Priest Sent by God

Detached Fresco (Stacco); Fragment
160 x 130 cm (Fragment)
167.5 x 136.5 cm (Stretcher)
Vatican Museums, inv. 40477

The picture area shows two scenes from the story which are given equal weight in the partition. On the left a palace crowned with battlements implies an urban setting in which the kneeling priest receives the charge from God, whose hand can still just be seen, to visit St. Benedict. In the right half that same priest is sitting in a rural environment with Benedict in front of his grotto and unpacks the food he has brought along.

The three haloed heads which appear at the bottom left do not belong to this scene. They are located in a strata of paintings which overlays that of the Benedict cycle, and which therefore belongs to a subsequent layer of paintings.

Lello da Orvieto

Benedict with Maurus and Placidus

Detached Fresco (Stacco); Fragment
67 x 133 cm (Fragment)
71 x 134.5 cm (Stretcher)
Vatican Museums, inv. 40465

The fragmentary condition of this fresco no longer allows identification this scene. Since, however, St. Benedict, kneeling in prayer, is shown with a beard, it is no longer a scene from his youth. It has been suggested that the two haloed monks standing behind him might be St. Placidus and St. Maurus, and the barely distinguishable facade of the church on the left might be the Monastery of Montecassino.

Lello da Orvieto

THE WAYWARD MONK AND THE DRAGON

Detached Fresco (Stacco); Fragment
166 x 159 cm (Fragment)
170 x 160 cm (Stretcher)
Vatican Museums, inv. 40469

The episode portrayed is taken from the *Dialoghi* of Gregory the Great. As in many of the other scenes in this cycle, the artist partitioned the composition into two sections of nearly equal size which he has subdivided by means of an architectural structure within the painting. This architectural element symbolizes the Rules of the Order from which the disobedient monk on the left is trying to escape. He is checked in this endeavor, however, by a dragon. His raised hands are at one and the same time the expression of fright as well as the pose of an *Orans,* or the prayerful. On the right, St. Benedict forgives the penitent who is kneeling before him, with the gentle laying on of the hand. The monks assisting him represent the fellowship into which the rebellious one has returned. The scene is highly symbolic.

Lello da Orvieto

BENEDICT RESURRECTS A MONK WHO HAD BEEN STRUCK AND KILLED BY A COLLAPSING WALL

Detached Fresco (Stacco); Fragment
116 x 86 cm (Fragment)
119.5 x 90.5 cm (Stretcher)
Vatican Museums, inv. 40474

In its original, undamaged condition this painting possessed an impressive monumental character derived from the size of the figures and the directness of its narrative element. In the part that remains, St. Benedict, identified by a halo, sits on the right before a tower in which the icon of an entreating Mother of God hangs. In front of him the hands of the resurrected monk can be recognized behind whom another monk lifts up the linen cloth in which the body had been wrapped.

Attributed to the Workshop of the Catherine Legend

Holy Princess with a Martyr's Crown

Detached Fresco (Stacco); Fragment
180 x 77 cm (Fragment)
187.5 x 83.5 cm (Stretcher)
Vatican Museums, inv. 40482

No specific information is so far available where this nearly life-sized figure was placed within St. Agnes; even the reference source, Martius Milesius Sarazanius, leaves ample room for speculation. The figure type and the framework suggest a gallery or procession of saints, as is known from early Christian and Byzantine contexts. Even the attribution of this figure to the workshop of the St. Catherine legend must be considered tentative.

Roman Workshop, approximately A.D. 1280-1300

St. Peter

Detached Fresco (Stacco); Fragment
148 x 69 cm (Fragment)
165.5 x 75.5 cm (Stretcher)
Vatican Museums, inv. 40484

The figure reminds one of the size
and framed presentation of the
holy princess. The difficulties
regarding an art—historical or
topographical correlation within
St. Agnes are very similar. But it has
a less schematic effect and shows a
different form of the halo, here in
relief. Also the application of color
seems to have been different; the
layer of paint is almost completely
gone, and only the brushed red
outline has survived. For that
reason the figure, otherwise clearly
of high quality, appears nearly
monochromatic or like a sinopia.
For all of these reasons it may not
have originated from the workshop
of the Catherine legend. It is
understandable why Lello da
Orvieto has been thought of, but
even in that case the stylistic
comparisons are not satisfactory.

Workshop of the Catherine Legend

St. Laurenzius

Detached Fresco (Stacco); Fragment
220 x 44 cm (Fragment)
234 x 70.5 cm (Stretcher)
Vatican Museums, inv. 40488

The long, light colored garment and the tonsorial hair style reveal that the young man is a deacon. In his left hand is a book which he needs for his duties, and in the lost right hand he held perhaps the martyr's palm. The instrument of his martyrdom, a flaming grate beneath his feet, allows this saint to be identified as the Roman Archdeacon Lawrence who often appears in association with St. Agnes. The nearly life-sized figure originated, along with other such fragments from St. Agnes, from a Gallery of Saints, even if the exact original location cannot be accurately ascertained. The facial type and the treatment of his vestment are very similar to those in the frescos of the Catherine legend. Therefore this fragment may also be regarded as belonging to the series of murals from that workshop.

Roman Workshop of Trecento

THREE MALE AND
TWO FEMALE SAINTS

Detached Fresco (Stacco); Fragment

145 x 205 cm
(Two fragments in their original
position; Fragments individually:
145 x 131 cm, and 85 x 52.5 cm);
160 x 217 cm (Stretcher)
Vatican Museums, inv. 40485

The composition of this fresco differs from the others since figures of various sizes appear here. A bearded saint seen from the front stands in the center with his right hand raised in blessing and a book in his left hand. Appearing on the left is a bishop with mitra also seen from the front and with a book in his left hand. The third figure, who likewise carries a book in the left hand, cannot be further identified because of the poor state of preservation. Between these large, probably male figures are two female saints on a substantially smaller scale, who are both symmetrically and compositionally associated with the large central figure. While the one on the right is identified by her crown and pearl-studded garment as a queen or princess, and could therefore portray St. Catherine of Alexandria in a Gallery of Saints, a book and a bundle of reeds (or rod, or martyr's palm) are insufficient for an identification of the one on the left.

Stylistically the fresco does not conform to either the Workshop of the Catherine legend or Lello da Orvieto without difficulties. Since parts of the two main cycles were at least partially painted over soon after they were completed (see inv. 40477), further investigation is also needed here to achieve a more accurate date and assignment.

Roman Workshop of Trecento

Two Saints

Detached Fresco (Stacco); Fragment
47 x 460 cm (Fragment)
56.5 x 184 cm (Stretcher)
Vatican Museums, inv. 40486

Only the heads of a holy bishop
and of an older, bearded saint have
survived from this painting. They
belonged to a Gallery of Saints
which was segmented by arcades
and rich cosmic decorations. The
figures look more flexible than the
holy princess (inv. 40482) and seem
in their slight rotation almost to
turn toward each other. Although
they are also depicted with their
halos in relief they seem more
strongly stylized than St. Peter
(inv. 40484). Perhaps they are to be
seen in the context of the strata of
overlaid paintings which occurred
soon after the cycles were
completed (compare inv. 40477).
Their original location within the
basilica has also not yet been
satisfactorily determined.

The thirteen fragments of frescoes, together with eleven more, are what remains of the old decoration of the crypt or "confession" of the church of San Nicola in Carcere.

The name of the Basilica is probably derived from the presence of a public prison (seventh-eighth centuries) in that area during the Byzantine age and from it being consecrated to Saint Nicholas, the bishop of Myra (Turkey) in the first half of the fourth century, one of the more venerated saints in the East and the West. He was called "of Bari" in memory of the city that hosted his remains after their transfer to Italy in 1087.

The first reliable news of the basilica, reported in the *Liber Pontificalis* (the title given to the anthology of the lives of the popes compiled from more diversified sources and composed during different times by different authors—the oldest collection dating back to the years between 514 and 523 and compiling the lives of the first popes in a single work) date back to the end of the eleventh century, although some scholars conjecture that its construction could date back to the seventh-eighth centuries (Proja, 1981, pp. 33-38; Pietrangeli, 1984, p. 20). The *Liber Pontificalis* (II, p. 295) asserts that in 1099, Urban II (1088-1099) "*apud Sanctum Nicolaum in carcere, in domo Petris Leonis, IIII Kal. Aug. Animam Deo reddidit,*" that is, the pontiff died on July 29 in the house of Pietro Leone near

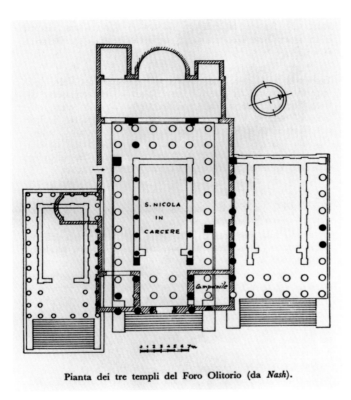

Pianta dei tre templi del Foro Olitorio (da *Nash*).

FIG. 1 *Basilica of San Nicola in Carcere, showing three contiguous ancient temples. (Figures in this chapter supplied by the author.)*

San Nicola in Carcere. The fact that the basilica was already defined in its title and in its appellation "in Carcere" during the years of the papacy of Urban II finds further confirmation in a plaque embedded in the right nave.

The church was built on the foundation of three contiguous temples of the ancient *Foro Olitorio*, a large square named for the market of vegetables and legumes (in Latin *holera*) held there since the period of the Roman republic. The central nave of the basilica occupied the area of the middle temple, while the lateral ones were erected in the space between one temple and the next, using the structures of the ancient buildings as the external walls (fig. 1).

Throughout the centuries, San Nicola in Carcere was subjected to various restructurings, beginning with that ordered by Pope Honorius II (1124-1130), whose work on the church was so extensive as to justify a new consecration of the building in 1128, as attested in a small plaque also embedded in the right nave. The basilica adopted the current design, was completely repainted, and was given a mosaic floor, a "*schola cantorum,*" a candelabrum for the Paschal candle, and a marble bishop's throne (fig 2.).

The following two major restorations took place under the titular Cardinal Rodrigo Borgia, elected pope with the name of Alexander VI (1492-1503), and under the Cardinal Federico Borromeo (1564-1631) at the end of the sixteenth century. The former, among other things, ordered the walling up of the access to the crypt or "confession" that would remain closed until the time of Cardinal Federico Borromeo. The latter, intending to reopen it to worship, subjected it to restoration after having it explored in 1591 by Alfonso Ciacconio, who wrote an accurate description, providing the first meaningful evidence of the medieval frescoes displayed here still on site (Biblioteca Apostolica Vaticana, *Vaticano Latino* 5409).

Unfortunately, in his report, the scholar only mentions the subjects of the paintings that were most likely distributed on "tria sacella parva" (three small chapels). In fact, in reference to the two figures of the pontiffs, Felix IV

FIG 2. *San Nicola in Carcere, showing ruins of the renovation of 1128.*

and Boniface IV, with the martyrs Abbondius, Abbondantius, Mark and Marcellian, and the prophets Moses, Jeremiah, Haggai, and Amos, a Flagellation of Christ and a Crucifixion, he makes no remarks as to the arrangement in their space and their possible relations with the rest of the decorative body.

We have more accurate information about the position of some frescoes in the eighteenth century due to the work of scholar Giovan Maria Crescimbeni who, describing the crypt and, more precisely, the small chapel to the left of the entrance, points out "above the vault of it, four prophets, Moses, Jeremiah, Haggai, and Amos ...and in the middle of them Christ who is baptized by Saint John the Baptist" (Crescimbeni, 1717, c. 262).

The frescoes were already in a state of decay at that time as one can infer from the report of the apostolic visitation of October 1721, in which the crypt is described as "adorned with sacred paintings, in large part damaged by antiquity and high humidity for which the marble altar is not covered except in years of celebration and in the holiday of Saint Nicholas" (Archivio Segreto Vaticano, *Sacra Congregazione, Visite Apostoliche* 118).

The paintings described by Crescimbeni, along with the other nineteen decorative fragments, are all that remain of the pictorial decoration of the crypt after the work of restoration of the church that led to the demolition of the crypt "dilapidated and crumbling" (Iacobini, 1989, p. 197) accomplished under Pius IX between 1853 and 1865.

The intervention was organized by the pontiff within a larger mission to "cultivate, through the care for the fine arts, the love of the Romans for religion and worship, promoting in them spiritual learning" (Pastorino, 1995, p. 51). This program of religious renewal entailed the restoration of many historic churches, among them San Nicola in Carcere. The efforts of the pope in forwarding this objective was efficaciously summarized by the academic architects Paolo Cacchiatelli and Gregorio Cleter: "Pius IX has caused, using in turn exhortation, incitement, and his own private money, the restoration, the renovation, the decoration of 48 churches in Rome alone,... His intention was our greater cultivation, our sanctification, the greater glory of God" (Pastorino, 1995, p. 51).

The twenty-four fragments, evidently considered the better preserved ones, were removed during the nineteenth-century restoration for the order of the Commissione Pontificia di Antichità e Belle Arti (Papal Commission for Antiquity and Fine Arts) that agreed to the construction of a new crypt that would be able to sustain the weight of the high altar. They did so with the condition that the ancient paintings "there preserved, were detached before the demolition and then reattached to the new structure" (Archivio di Stato di Roma, Ministero del Commercio, Industria e Agricoltura, Belle Arti e lavori pubblici, sez. V, tit. I, art. 1, busta 359/6: letter of February 10, 1855). The recovery of these paintings took place, therefore, with the precise goal of "recomposing the painting of the entire vault" after the renovation of the crypt, "putting back the same fragments in their place and adding, by a hand skillful at such work, the little that is missing" (Servi, April 13, 1854).

The *stacco* of the frescoes was completed by architect Gapare Servi under the direction of Pellegrino Succi, famous during that period for that type of procedure and who, already in 1854, had transferred them to canvas and had them stored. Because of financial difficulties, however, the project of replacement did not take place and it was decided that it would be better to display the frescoes in the Lateran Museum, where they would remain until 1926 when they were taken to the Vatican. They were restored for the first time in 1930-31; and again between 1972 and 1983, when a new intervention on most of the fragments was ordered and they were applied on a support of *termanto* (material previously called cadorite). Yet another restoration of the fragments, that involved, among other things, the placement of the remaining pieces on a termanto support, was finished last year in preparation for the current exhibit.

While the description by Crescimbeni allows for the situation of the prophets Moses, Jeremiah, Haggai, and Amos, and of the Baptism of Christ on the vault of the left chapel, it is still very difficult to ascertain the position of the other nineteen frescoes. With relative certainty, one can in fact only hypothesize that the fragments with the pheasants and the hare were part of the decoration of the vault because of the presence of the same border on the tondos and the central medallion, and that the series of the birds, resting on floral elements within intersecting circles, belonged to the ornamentation of the base, given their clear affinity with the wainscot below the *Stories of Saint Alexius* in the lower church of San Clemente.

The paintings, in fresco over a plaster of lime and pozzuolana, were refined with a whitening of lime and marble power. Recent criticism places the works stylistically within the Roman painting of the first quarter of the twelfth century. In fact, after the nineteenth-century attribution of the works to "the early times of Christian painting" (Servi, June 8, 1855) and later to the end of the twelfth century by Van Marle (1921, p. 185; 1923, I, p. 187) based on the comparison of the tondos with those of Santa Croce in Gerusalemme, a more accurate analysis was achieved at the end of the 1920s with Golzio (s.d., p. 51) who connected the completion of the frescoes to the restructuring of the building with the new consecration of the church in 1128.

This thesis was taken up again at the beginning of the 1950s by Garrison (1957-1958, p.183-194), who placed the fragments within the Roman historic and artistic context of the first half of the twelfth century, connecting them, in particular, with two other works: the codex E.16 of the Biblioteca Vallicelliana and the Triptych of the Savior in Tivoli. However, it is because of Toubert (1970) that we begin to understand the individuation of the strongly archaeological character of the paintings that "must be framed with full rights in that phase of fervid and aware 'renouveau paléochrétien' (early Christian renewal) that imprints Roman painting since the beginning of the twelfth century and finds in the frescoes of Santa Maria in Cosmedin first (1123) and in the mosaic of San Clemente later, the other two leading monuments of the current (Iacobini, 1989, p. 199)."

There are, in fact, many motifs of early Christian descent purposefully inserted in the cycle of San Nicola, from the birds on the branches in blossom to the peacocks of the lunettes to the dolphins and the garlands, that in their brightness of color are reminiscent of the ancient mosaics. However, it is not just the simple renewal of single ornamental elements, but rather an intellectual recovery that pervades the whole pictorial project from the general organization to the use of color to the style of the execution.

—Anna Maria De Strobel

REFERENCES

Wolfgang Fritz Volbach. *I dipinti dal X secolo a Giotto*, Città del Vaticano 1979, pp. 33-42.

Richard Krautheimer. *Rome—Profile of a City, A.D. 312-1308*, Princeton 1980, pp. 24-26, 68, 85, 87, 93, 191, and 248.

Serena Romano. *I cicli a fresco di Sant' Agnese fuori le mura*, in: Fragmenta picta—Affreschi e mosaici staccati del Medioevo romano, eds. Maria Andaloro, Alessandra Ghidoli, Antonio Iacobini, Serena Romano and Alessandro Tomei, Rome 1990, pp. 245-258.

Serena Romano. *Eclissi di Roma— Pittura murale a Roma e nel Lazio da Bonifacio VIII a Martino V (A.D. 1295-1431*, Rome 1992, pp. 9-10, 15-19, 35-45 and 170-174 (with the citations of the older literature).

Armanda e Laura Pastorino. *L restauri delle chiese ad impianto basilicale a Roma durante il pontificato di Pio IX*, in: Recerche di Storia dell'Arte XCVI, 1996, pp. 61-71.

Arnold Nesselrath. *The Frescoes from Sant' Agnese fuori le mura*, in: Medieval Frescoes from the Vatican Museums, Catalog of the Exhibit in the Toyota Municipal Museum of Art from 8th September to 8th November 1998, ed. Nosa Yoko, Toyota 1998, pp. 9-10.

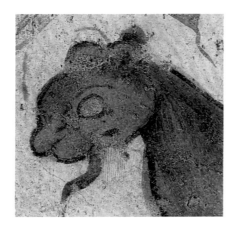

Roman School, circa 1128

PROPHET HAGGAI

Fresco on termanto,
diameter 59.5 cm.
Vatican Museums, inv. 40515

Prophet Haggai, identifiable by the
name written on the sides of the
halo, holds in his hands a scroll
with the biblical citation "IL (sic)
LOCO ISTO DABO/PACEM DICIT
D(OMI)N(U)S" (In this place I will
grant peace, declares the Lord;
Haggai 2, 9). This is the final verse
of the paragraph in which Haggai
announces the coming of the
Messiah, who with His presence
will sanctify the new temple of
Jerusalem. Haggai, in fact, carried
out his prophetic mission during
the second year of the reign of
Darius (520 B.C.), urging the Jews
to rebuild the temple that had been
destroyed seventy years before. The
figure of the prophet is highlighted
over a red background surrounded
by a garland of flowers, fruit, and
leaves over a black background.

The fresco was restored and
applied on a termanto support
in 1977.

Roman School, circa 1128
PROPHET JEREMIAH

Fresco on termanto,
diameter 59.5 cm.
Vatican Museums, inv. 40506

Jeremiah, whose name is written
on the sides of his face, holds in his
hands a scroll with the biblical
citation "[...]CO QUASI AGNUS
MAB/[SUET]US QUI PORTATUR"
(I was like a gentle lamb led to
the slaughter; Jeremiah 11, 19).
The excerpt, which speaks of the
plot against Jeremiah in Anatot, is a
clear allusion to Christ and his
sacrifice on the cross.

The medallion is surrounded, like
the others, by a perimetric band of
fruit and leaves on a black
background.

The fresco was restored and
applied on a termanto support
in 1977.

Roman School, circa 1128

PROPHET AMOS

Fresco on termanto, diameter 59.5cm.
Vatican Museums, inv. 40513

The prophet, whose name appears
on the sides of the halo, is
portrayed in an almost frontal
position, holding in his hands a
scroll with the biblical citation
"ECCE D(OMI)N(U)S EXERCITU/UM
GRADIENS" (The Lord, the God of
hosts is his name; Amos 4, 13) that
alludes to Christ and the
Ascension. The verse is drawn from
a section of the Book of Amos in
which the prophet announces the
destruction of the kingdom of
Israel, the exile of its people, and, as
the only means of salvation, the
observance of the law of God.

The medallion is surrounded, like
the others, by a perimetric band
with flowers and fruit.

The fresco was restored and
applied on a termanto support
in 1977.

Roman School, circa 1128

DECORATIVE FRAGMENT WITH
VASE AND TWO DOLPHINS
FACING EACH OTHER

Fresco on termanto, 45.3 x 63 cm.
Vatican Museums, inv. 40512

This gray vase is decorated with
undulating blue lines, and a rich
bunch of leaves, fruit, and flowers
represents the central motif of the
fragment, delimited at the bottom
by an ochre stripe bordered by two
red lines, and at the top by a blue
band. The latter leads to the
supposition that the fragment was
connected to the one portraying a
green dolphin (inv. 40499, not
displayed) or another similar one. In
the lateral spaces, the decoration is
composed of two figs of the tonality
of the background outlined with a
dark line, by two green dolphins
with red shades, and by a few green
leaves spread on the surface.

The fresco was restored and
applied on a termanto support in
1983 and in the last restoration was
made uniform in the treatment of
the background.

Roman School, circa 1128

DECORATIVE FRAGMENT WITH WINGED DRAGON

Fresco on termanto, 39.5 x 77 cm.
Vatican Museums, inv. 40495

A winged dragon with a feline head and an eel-like body, surrounded by a few green leaves, is highlighted on the light-colored background at the center of the lunette, delimited by a band bordered with blue. An elegant ornamental motif composed of blue and yellow flowers with green leaves completes the decoration.

The fresco was restored and applied on a termanto support in 1998 and in the last restoration was made uniform in the treatment of the background.

Roman School, circa 1128

DECORATIVE FRAGMENT WITH PEACOCK

Fresco on termanto, 21.5 x 41.8 cm.
Vatican Museums, inv. 40498

The decorative motif is represented by a lunette delimited around its perimeter by a dark brown line and an ochre band with a peacock with a dark brown body and green wings turned to the left at the center. The decoration is completed by two red rosettes and a green leaf.

The fresco was restored and applied on a termanto support in 2000.

Roman School, circa 1128

Decorative Fragment with Pheasant

Fresco on termanto, 39 x 50.3 cm.
Vatican Museums, inv. 40489

The fragment portrays a bird in
profile, probably a pheasant,
between two branches with leaves
and flowers. The white background
of the plaster serves as a base for
the coloring of the feathering,
rendered with the addition of
brush-strokes in a red earth color
for the head, the chest, and the tail,
and in black for the rest of the
body, while the wings, the legs, and
the beak are painted in yellow.

   The fresco was restored and
applied on a termanto support in
1981 and in the last restoration was
made uniform in the treatment of
the background.

Roman School, circa 1128

DECORATIVE FRAGMENT
WITH BIRD

Fresco on termanto, 47.5 x 65.2 cm.
Vatican Museums, inv. 40514

The decorative motif is represented
by a bird, identifiable with a crane
or a heron, inside a triangular space
delimited by a dark brown line and
an ochre band. The bird is
portrayed with the red-orange
body resting on a stylized raceme
with a green stem and red flowers.
Three red rosettes are painted on
the light background of the plaster.
According to L. Magnani
("Rendiconti della Pontificia
Accademia Romana
d'Archeologia," VIII, 1932, p. 243),
this fragment, together with
inv. 40507 (not displayed),
represents the decoration of a
corbel of the vault.

The fresco was restored and
applied on a termanto support
in 2000.

Roman School, circa 1128

DECORATIVE FRAGMENT WITH BIRD

Fresco on termanto, 35.5 x 45 cm.
Vatican Museums, inv. 40490

The central motif of the fragment is represented by a bird with open wings and a little tuft of feathers on its head, resting on a branch in blossom, and turned to the right with its head turned towards its back. The small scene is enclosed in a circle intersecting four other semicircles, creating a decoration that, developing both vertically and horizontally, must have represented with some other fragments, the ornamentation of the wainscot of one of the walls of the crypt. We can infer this from its similarity with what we find below the *Stories of Saint Alexius* in the lower basilica of San Clemente in Rome.

The fresco was restored and applied on a termanto support in 1983; upon the last restoration, it was detached from its support again and applied to a new one of the same size as that of the other five fragments with the same subject (inv. 40491, 40492, 40502, 40503, 40504).

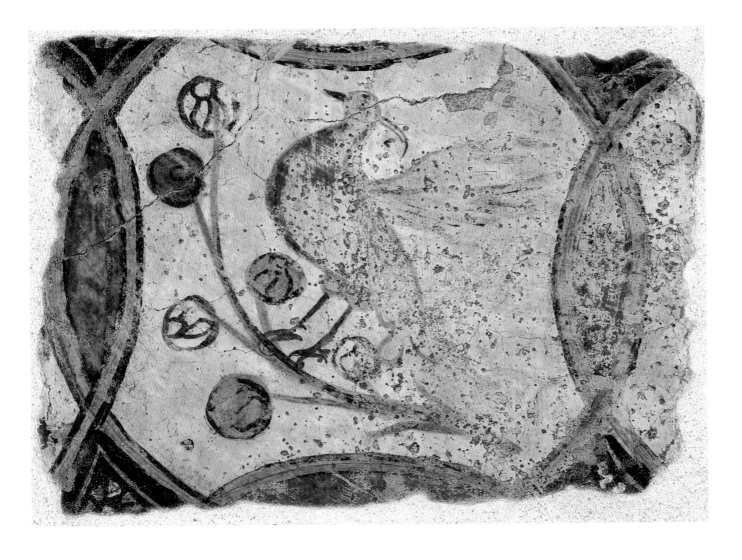

Roman School, circa 1128

DECORATIVE FRAGMENT
WITH BIRD

Fresco on termanto, 35.5 x 45 cm.
Vatican Museums, inv. 40492

The fragment presents the same
ornamental motif of inv. 40490,
represented by a circle intersecting
four semicircles. The bird that
occupies the center of the
composition is different however.
It is probably a lapwing with blue
body, wings, and tail, turned to the
left, and resting on a branch in
blossom.

The fresco was restored and
applied on a termanto support in
1983; upon the last restoration it
was detached from its support
again and applied to a new one of
the same size as that of the other
five fragments with the same
subject (inv. 40491, 40490, 40502,
40503, 40504).

Roman School, circa 1128

DECORATIVE FRAGMENT WITH VASE AND TWO BIRDS

Fresco on termanto, 38 x 64 cm.
Vatican Museums, inv. 40493

The lunette is delimited at the bottom by a brown border and at the top by a festoon, interrupted at the center, with fruit in green and orange on a black background. Two dark brown birds with yellow wings, at the sides of a vase from which white and blue flowers emerge, appear in the middle, on the light background of the plaster.

The fresco was restored and applied on a termanto support in 2000.

Roman School, circa 1128

DECORATIVE FRAGMENT
WITH VASE AND TWO BIRDS

Fresco on termanto, 41.5 x 73.2 cm.
Vatican Museums, inv. 40505

The fragment, whose decoration is
very similar to that of inv. 40493, is
composed by a lunette delimited by
a festoon interrupted at the top,
with fruit and leaves in green and
orange on a black background. At
the center, two birds in a dark
brown color with yellow wings and
flowers in their beaks rest at the
sides of a big vase from which
white and blue flowers emerge.
The fresco was restored and applied
on a termanto support in 2000.

Roman School, circa 1128

DECORATIVE FRAGMENT WITH MASK AND TWO DOLPHINS

Fresco on termanto, 40.5 x 55 cm.
Vatican Museums, inv. 40501

A mask surrounded by a garland decorated with red circles and triangles, with two dolphins facing each other, represent the dominant motif of the fragment. On the light background of the plaster, there are also two small garlands with a red-brown rosette at the center and four rosettes placed around the mask.

FIG. 1. *Interior of the Basilica of San Paolo in ruins: etching from the collection "Le antichità romane" edited by Luigi Rossini. (Figures for this chapter supplied by the author.)*

While on a trip to Italy in 1740, the versatile scholar Charles de Brosses[1] explained with wonder and abundant detail how the mosaicists of the Basilica of Saint Peter managed to: "...take the fresco paintings off the wall, detaching the back surface without spoiling the painting..."[2] Thus, it is clear that the technique of *stacco a massello* (block detachment), that is, the cut and removal of the whole structure of plaster and wall that sustains the fresco, was widely practiced at that time.[3] Although the description of the operation— faithfully reported by de Brosses[4]— raised some questions, the *stacco a massello* method represented the only alternative to the destruction of entire cycles of frescoes.[5] The choice to "destroy or conserve" was often the end result of an evaluation that responded to precise circumstances of specific historic epochs.[6] The *stacco* was also frequently used for needs related to the change of function or the restructuring of entire buildings. For example, the eighteenth-century restructuring of the church of SS. Apostoli in Rome with the destruction of the majestic fresco in the apse of the Ascension of Christ by Melozzo da Forlì (fig. 1) employed this technique. On that occasion, only ten images[7] were spared, primarily due to the intercession of some enlightened persons.[8] For further confirmation of this way of thinking, we can still make use of the words of Monsieur de Brosses about his "insane" intentions concerning even Raphael's paintings in the Stanze Vaticane: "...At this point it is not difficult for me to understand why I cannot remove the frescoes, which would not be fit for a similar process; however, it is true that sometimes a first discovery causes another one. If this ever occurred, you can be sure that I would ruin myself making projects on the Vatican, on the Palazzo del Tè, on the frescoes by Raphael and Giulio Romano."[9] Still, in some cases *stacco* was not even used, as on the occasion of the fire of the Basilica of San Paolo in 1823. In fact, drawings and etchings of the period demonstrate the high percentage of frescoes of inestimable value that escaped catastrophe and that would later be destroyed to allow for the construction of the new Basilica (fig. 2). *Stacco* was also practiced for devotional reasons or, as we will see later, more simply by collectors.[10] At the beginning of the eighteenth century, a real method of taking only the pictorial pellicle, termed *strappo* (pull) of the color, was discovered. A fragment obtained in such way could be applied to a canvas that was stretched on a wooden frame and properly framed. In that period, the possibility of obtaining these kinds of easel paintings satisfied the incessant demand of the antiquarian market that led to an unregulated supply of fragments

FIG. 2. *Angelo Musicante (Musician Angel) by Melozzo da Forlì, before the last restoration. The insertion of the fragment within a frame is an example of turning a fresco into an easel painting.*

preservation would lead in time to the formation and evolution of the current "preservation consciousness" that, although ambiguous for many centuries, was rarely dictated by a true desire to safeguard the artwork.

The fact that the removal of artwork of past centuries was seen as the only viable alternative to the destruction of important paintings, can be justified by the exiguity of the technical and scientific resources of the time. Today however, there are no longer any excuses for the extreme solution of the *stacco* or *strappo* methods. Until a few years ago, before the concept of "prevention" was finally accepted, fragments—if not entire cycles of frescoes—were taken away from their historic and artistic contexts in order to resolve the issue of the environmental problems of their unhealthy original location.[12] Nowadays, on the contrary, in compliance with the directions issued in the Carta del Restauro (Charter of Restoration) of 1972, inspired by the principles exposed in the Teoria del Restauro (Theory of Restoration) by Cesare Brandi,[13] extreme solutions can be adopted only when very complex interventions of preservation (like the *stacco*) represent the sole alternative to the loss of adaptation and traditional layout of the mural paintings. In these cases, the removal of seriously damaged frescoes can be more readily justified as it represents the only option to preserve them in safer places.

Due to extremely advanced technology, we can now effect accurate preliminary monitoring of environmental restorations, while structural engineering is now able to provide different solutions for the static restoration of buildings.

Techniques of Intervention and Evolution of the Material

Today, in the very rare cases in which it is necessary to remove the mural paintings, we employ the *stacco*, more rarely the *strappo*, and even more infrequently the *stacco a massello*. The latter is used only when the first two methods are not viable because of the precarious conditions of the plaster and walls.

The necessary operations to execute a *stacco a massello* are incredibly complex and involve the employment of many workers with different specializations. After adequately protecting the painting—an operation common to all three methods of mural removal—the section of the wall to be removed is cut on its four sides in order to allow for the insertion of wooden boards. This sort of cage allows the wall to be lifted by mechanical gear and to be transported to suitable premises where

of frescoes that were extremely marketable due to the lightness provided by the *strappo* method. Later, probably due to the obstacles in finding these pieces and the difficulty in removing the work perfectly intact, the figure of the forger appeared. Forgers focused their efforts on works in plaster that were sold as fragments of supposed famous paintings of the Renaissance.[11] As centuries passed, the first tentative efforts at a preservation method were introduced. The *stacco* represented the only way to safeguard works that risked being ruined. Paintings that showed signs of decay because of bad environmental conditions were removed and transferred to an unrelated context. The introduction of methods of the thickness of the wall could be reduced to that of a normal detached fresco.

Stacco, instead, means the removal of only the plaster and the painted surface. It is also necessary to protect the painted surface by gluing to it two cloths: the first made of cotton muslin or *velatino*, and the second made of linen or *tela pattina*. A major concern is in applying the cloths as uniformly as possible, avoiding air bubbles that would prevent an homogeneous detachment of the fresco. Before starting, if the area to be detached is not flat, a controforma (counterform) for containment is constructed to preserve all the irregularities of the painted surface. In this way, the operator can intervene without risking the loss of the original shape and features of the painting. When the glue is completely dry, the fresco is detached beginning at one of the upper corners with the insertion of a long blade between wall and plaster. After the detachment, the fresco is turned to reduce the thickness of the plaster on the back to a few millimeters (fig. 3) and one or more *velatini* are applied to the back with very liquid grout. Once dry, the protective cloths are removed and the fresco is ready to be applied on a new, lighter, more resistant support. When the original form of the pictorial fragment follows a particular architectonic structure (web, niche, vault, etc.), it is advisable to create a structure that allows for the reconstruction of the original form. In this case, contrary to what normally occurs in the procedure, it is not the fresco that is applied to the new support, but rather a separately modeled structure that is made to adhere as an exact imprint of the back of the painting.

As for the *strappo*, the preliminary phases are the same as those employed for the stacco; however, the goal of the operation is the removal of the painted surface alone. When the adhesive is dry, an edge of the cloth is raised and gradually placed onto rollers as the color is removed from the wall. Removing the pictorial surface alone can lead to the discovery of the original preparatory drawing, the sinopia, underneath.[14] In fresco painting, the sinopia offers insight into the artist's original ideas in the division of the entire composition. Apart from the abuse of the *strappo* in the past, the recovery of preparatory drawings has allowed for the acquisition of useful technical data for the study of art history.

The adhesive shared by the three methods of removal is an animal glue known as *colla forte*, and it is employed with different purposes.[15] In the *strappo*, its function is to produce an effect comparable to that of a giant piece of scotch tape and therefore must be used in its maximum concentration. In the two kinds of

FIG. 3. *Back of a detached fresco.*

stacco on the contrary, the gluing of the cloths has simply a protective purpose, and thus it is sufficient to use a more diluted solution, for example, with the addition of molasses, which, as a natural plastic-coating substance, reduces its power of contraction.[16] Among the techniques of restoration, the removal of frescoes by the three described typologies has remained virtually unaltered throughout the centuries and still follows the same operational stages: protection, removal, and transfer of the painting to a new supportive structure. The major innovations that have been introduced have been in the fields of research and the execution of new supports for the reassembling of *stacchi* or *strappi* of frescoes. The new supports, the products of a more modern conception, respond more effectively to more recent preservation issues.

Restoration of the Frescoes of Sant'Agnese fuori le Mura and San Nicola in Carcere in Rome

Following the historical and methodological traditions mentioned above, we have to consider the older restorations of the frescoes coming from the Roman churches of Sant'Agnese fuori le Mura and San Nicola in Carcere from their detachment from their original surroundings to the current preservation works carried out by the Laboratorio Restauro Pitture (Laboratory for the Restoration of Paintings) of the Vatican Museums.

All the frescoes were removed during the nineteenth century, more precisely, the first in 1853 and the others in 1855 (fig. 4.) Pellegrino Succi was the person responsible for overseeing the removals and it is interesting to pause for a moment on the "professional history" of this restorer because it emphasizes how the technique of the *stacco* was disseminated and used in the not too remote past.

Pellegrino Succi belonged to a true dynasty of restorers. His father, Giacomo, was called to Rome by Pope Pius VI (Giovanni Braschi, 1775-1779), to carry out the *stacco* of some mural paintings at Palazzo Corsini before its destruction. Giacomo was among the first Italian restorers to perfect the technique of *stacco* and *strappo*. The result of his first work in Rome was so successful that the pontiff, sensing the possibility of "easy profits" for the Roman aristocracy and to better safeguard the artistic heritage of the city, nominated Giuseppe Succi "extractor of the Sacred Apostolic Palace" assigning to him a monthly pension for life with one stipulation: Succi was not to effect works of *stacco* and *strappo* on someone else's behalf in the Papal States without the specific authorization of the Pontiff himself.[17] His sons, Domenico and Pellegrino, became very skillful heirs of their father's tradition, so much so that Pellegrino acquired the same pension after the death of his father in 1809. Pellegrino personally oversaw the removal of the frescoes of Sant'Agnese and San Nicola as well as those of the Niccolina Chapel of Beato Angelico in the Vatican and of the Basilica of San Paolo Fuori le Mura. He also removed the Etruscan paintings of the "François Tomb" in Vulci and, between 1844 and 1855, he worked with his other brother Giovanni on the restoration of the Basilica of Assisi.

The events that led to the detachment of the paintings of Sant'Agnese are well-known and well-documented. During a visit by Pope Pius IX in 1855, the Pope was involved in a cave-in, but escaped miraculously unharmed. The restoration of the entire monastic complex in memory of that event was then organized. The work was assigned to architect A. Busiri Vici and during the general architectonic restructuring, some paintings—two pictorial cycles, one of the "Stories from the life of Saint Catherine of Alexandria" and the other of the "Stories from the life of Saint Benedict," as well as many isolated figures of saints and martyrs— were found under the layers of scialbi.[18] These were detached by Pellegrino Succi, and were restored and displayed at the Museo Lateranense until 1926 when they became part of the collection of the Pinacoteca Vaticana.

The vicissitudes concerning the detachment of the small fragments of fresco at San Nicola in Carcere are less clear and known. They were most probably originally from the crypt and were also found during the "architectonic restoration" of the building, that had begun with the more general recovery of the remains of early Christian religious art during the papacy of Pius IX.

FIG. 4. *Fresco detached from Sant'Agnese Fuori le Mura representing Saint Lawrence: the photo shows the condition of the fragment before the current restoration.*
FIG. 5. *Saint Lawrence, the photo shows the wooden frame applied in 1855 and the plaster of the intervention of 1926.*

They too were restored and followed the same destiny as the paintings of Sant'Agnese.

After their removal, the thickness of the remains of the original plaster on the back of all frescoes was reduced till it became, in some cases, completely lost. Glued onto a large-weave canvas using an adhesive composed presumably of *colla forte* and casein, they were then mounted, stretching the canvas, on a fir frame and did not undergo any other aesthetic intervention. After their arrival at the Vatican Museums, the first restoration of the frescoes was organized in 1930-1931, as the loss of tension of the canvas compromised their preservation. The supports were not replaced but, after the application of a second canvas (only for the paintings of Sant'Agnese), the canvasses of all the fragments were stiffened by applying an adhesive mixture composed of "carpenter's glue and plaster" (fig. 5) to the back of them. This was followed by the wide puttying of plaster and glue to make up for the many defective areas, both protecting the original margins and allowing a greater "readability" of the paintings. Finally, according to the aesthetic use of the time, extensive repainting was done on the puttying and on the original color. Since that restoration, no other work has been done on the frescoes.

When, at the beginning of 2000, our Laboratories began the most recent restoration, the panels were in a similar state as that in the 1930s. In fact, the low tension of the canvas on the wooden support, worsened even more by the deformations suffered by the frame itself, did not guarantee the adhesion of the pictorial surface to the underlying supporting layers any longer. The remains of glues and other substances used in the past also presented a further serious element of decay. It was decided therefore to replace the old wooden frames with modern material defined with precise physical and chemical characteristics.

The Laboratorio Restauro Pitture of the Vatican Museums boasts an old tradition concerning the precise technical practice of transferring mural paintings onto new supports, a tradition that has been strengthened throughout the decades and that has led to the use of cadorite (now termed *termanto*) today[19]. The properties of this material are mainly in their guarantee of reversibility, lightness, and mechanical protection. In addition, it presents a coefficient of thermal expansion not so different from that of the pictorial surface, and an excellent resistance to atmospheric and biologic agents and solvents—all characteristics responding to the requirements for the optimum intervention for a correct preservation.

The frescoes of Sant'Agnese fuori le Mura and San Nicola in Carcere have been reapplied on supports of cadorite reinforced with structural anodized aluminum. The modern intervention to transfer the paintings onto new supports started with the protection of the painted surface with *velatini* to allow for the safe removal of the two canvasses from the back (fig. 6).

The next step then was to use a scalpel to reduce the old thickness slowly and precisely, completely removing the adhesive mixture on the back of the fragments. The removal of layers of the old mixture allowed for a consolidation of the color that, being made from the back, offered a greater guarantee of adherence to the new support. The frescoes, however, were not applied directly onto the cadorite support: an intermediate layer composed of a mixture of plaster, covered on both sides with *velatino*, was sandwiched between them. This "sandwich," usually termed the "intervention's layer," can be considered a sort of diaphragm between the original materials of the fresco and the new support. In the case of future necessity, it also allows for the separation of the original painting from the modern support without any damage. In the case of these frescoes, the mixture of grout also provided a new and concrete thickness to the thin original pictorial film, and gave the painting structure further solidity.

Once the fragments were placed onto the new supports and the paintings were properly cleansed, the restorers decided to maintain them at a higher level than the surface on which they are laid and "glued." This solution has allowed for the aesthetic treatment of the bottom of the frescoes that suggests, because of the materials and the superficial treatment, the original wall substratum upon which the frescoes were painted (fig. 7). Finally, the chromatic reintegration, accomplished with the maximum respect for the original painting, has been defined within the more general preservation criteria that inspired the restoration. This has helped to provide a hypothesis of spatiality that allowed for an aesthetic and historic reading of the images as close as possible to what had been the original situation of the cycle within its environmental context.[20]

—Maurizio De Luca

ENDNOTES
[1] Charles de Brosses, president for life of the Parliament of Bourgoigne (Digione 1709-Paris 1777), was a versatile scholar of history, archeology, geography, and linguistics.
[2] C. de Brosses, *Viaggio in Italia*, Rome, 1973, Letter XLVIII, p. 481.
[3] The tradition of *stacco a massello* can already be found in the time of classical antiquity. Pliny and Vitruvius narrate, in fact, how fragments of the mural painting of Sparta was transferred to Rome

FIG. 6. *Saint Lawrence, back: the phase in which the cloth and plaster are removed.*

FIG. 7. *Saint Lawrence, after its application on a new support after the restoration.*

(*Naturalis Historia* libro XXXV and *De architectura* libro II). News of this practice can also be found during the Renaissance when the operation of cutting the walls was habitually entrusted to a sculptor whose technical abilities would prevent inopportune fracturing of the artwork.

[4] "…how they could remove the fresco paintings from the wall, detaching the wall behind without damaging the picture. After having literally broken the wall along all its length, they fixed some beams on one side as a frame and the same thing is done on the other side as well as along the top. When everything is stable, fixed, and pressed with iron levers, it is lifted in order to be able to cut the bottom and apply the fourth corner of the frame. Then, it is all removed and transferred using machines."
C. de Brosses, *Viaggio*, cit., Lettera XLVIII, p. 481.

[5] Even Michelangelo did not hesitate to destroy the frescoes by Perugino on the wall of the altar of the Sistine Chapel in order to paint his *Last Judgement*.

[6] In turn, the same *Last Judgement* risked being destroyed in 1564 when the order came to remove all those paintings in the churches that contained obscene images or images which did not conform to the regulations of the Council of Trent.

[7] The thirteen visages of *Angels* and *Apostles* are conserved in the Pinacoteca Vaticana, and the *Redemptor* is at the Palazzo del Quirinale.

[8] "…Taja, describing them in the chapter house of Saint Peter's, specifies that they were saved due also to his intervention and that of Father Sebastiano Resta, the noted collector of drawings." A.

Conti in *Storia del Restauro e della conservazione delle opere d'arte*, Milano 1973, cap.V, p. 118.

[9] C. de Brosses, *Viaggio* cit., Lettera XLVIII, p. 482.

[10] In some cases, sacred images considered miraculous were moved from the places they were found and placed in the centers of new churches dedicated to them.

[11] Approximately 25 years ago, Federico Zeri, called "Forger in Calcinaccio," the author of a series of forgeries in plaster. In 1994, G. Mazzoni definitively identified him as the forger from Siena, Umberto Giunti (1886-1970).

[12] It is the case of the Etruscan frescoes of the Tomb of Francois di Vulci that were removed in 1863 due to high humidity and the formation of concretions on the surface of the painting, and were subjected to further intervention by transferring them to hempen cloth in 1947. In 1987, certain fragments preserved at the Villa Albani in Rome, were definitively mounted on panels of Aerolam (a *sandwich* constituted of nests of bees between two layers of glass wool and polyester resin and hardened by an anodized aluminum structure) and restored, under my supervision, at the Laboratorio di Restauro dei Musei Vaticani on the occasion of the exhibit for the 150th anniversary of the Museo Gregoriano Etrusco.

[13] Cesare Brandi (Siena 1906-Vignano 1988) was an art critic and founder of the Istituto Centrale del Restauro.

[14] The word derives from the term "Sinopis," a red earth with a base of oxidized iron, already known by the Romans and the Greeks and coming from the ancient city of Sinope on the Black Sea. The color was used to trace the first sketch of the composition on *arriccio*, that is, on that plaster layer that came in direct contact with the wall upon which was applied the plaster for the application of the fresco pigments.

[15] Other terms of the animal *colla forte: colla cervione, colla di Zurigo, colla da falegname*.

[16] Molasses is a dense, brown , sweet liquid that is the residue of the refinement of sugar.

[17] Term commonly used at the time to describe a restorer specialized in "extractions" (*stacchi* and *strappi*) of mural paintings.

[18] *Scialbo* is the covering layer (commonly of lime) applied in the course of the centuries on the paintings generally for hygienic motives after the plague.

[19] Cadorite is an expanded material that has been used at the Laboratorio Restauro Dipinti dei Musei Vaticani, since the end of the 1960s.

[20] The intervention has been executed by restorer Fabio Piacentini of the Laboratorio Restauro Pitture dei Musei Vaticani who served as director for the work group composed by F. Prantera with the collaboration of F. Leopardini, a contract worker, and restorers F. Cantisani, B. Marocchini, and S. Zucconi who served as external collaborators in charge of the restoration, following the directions provided, on five of the fragments inv. 40476, 40481, 40485, 40494, 40516.
The supports for the paintings have been constructed by M. Alesi and M. Mattarocci of the Laboratio Restauro Manufatti Lignei dei Musei Vaticani; the photographic documentation has been executed by F. Bono, A. Bracchetti, L. Giordano, D. Pivato, and P. Zigrossi of the Laboratorio Fotografico dei Musei Vaticani. The system of suspension of the paintings has been overseen by the firm F. De Simone, Rome.

REFERENCES
De Brosses C., *Viaggio in Italia,* Roma, 1973.
Maltese C., *Le tecniche artistiche*, Milano, 1973.
Conti A., *Storia del restauro,* Milano, 1973.
Bandi C., *Teoria del Restauro*, Torino, 1977.
ICR - DIMOS, parte I, modulo 1, *Tecniche di esecuzione e materiali costitutivi*, Roma, 1978.
W.F.Volbach, *Catalogo della Pinacoteca Vaticana*, Vol. I, Città del Vaticano, 1979.
E.U.A. Novara, 1980.
AA.VV., *La fabbrica dei colori*, Roma, 1988.
Conti A., *Storia del restauro e della conservazione delle opere d'arte*, Milano, 1988.
Basile G., *Che cos'è il restauro*, Roma, 1989.
Perusini G., *Il restauro dei dipinti e delle sculture lignee*, Udine, 1989
Maltese C., *I supporti nelle arti pittoriche* , Milano, 1990.
Conti A., *Manuale del restauro*, Torino, 1996.

APPENDIX

HISTORICAL FIGURES AND EVENTS IN ROME FROM THE TWELFTH TO THE FOURTEENTH CENTURY

1143-1144	pope Celestine II Guido, from Città di Castello
1144-1145	pope Lucius II Gerardo Caccianemici dell'Orso, from Bologna
1145-1153	pope Eugenius III Bernardo Paganelli, from Montemagno
1153-1154	pope Anastasius IV Corrado, from Rome
1154-1159	pope Adrian IV Nicholas Breakspeare, English
1159-1181	pope Alexander III Rolando Bandinelli, from Siena
1159 to 1180	series of antipopes
1181-1185	pope Lucius III Ubaldo Allucignoli, from Lucca
1185-1187	pope Urban III Uberto Crivelli, from Milan
1187	pope Gregorius VIII Alberto de Morra, from Benevento
1187-1191	pope Clement III Paolino Scolare, from Rome
1191-1198	pope Celestine III Giacinto Borbone Orsini, from Rome recognized the autonomy of the Commune.
1198-1216	pope Innocent III Lotario dei Conti di Segni, from Anagni
1216-1227	pope Honorius III Cencio Savelli, Roman
1227-1241	pope Gregorius IX Ugolino dei Conti di Segni, from Anagni
1241	pope Celestine IV Goffredo Castiglione, from Milan
1243-1254	pope Innocent IV Sinibaldo Fieschi dei Conti di Lavagna, from Genoa

1143-1145
Installation of the Roman Senate and recognition of the Roman Commune by pope Eugenius III in 1145

1153
Agreement between Anastasius IV and Frederick Barbarossa to support the temporal power of the papacy.

1155-1167
The Roman Senate offered the imperial crown to Frederick Barbarossa who refused it. He would later accept it from Pope Adrian IV, who crowned him on July 1155 in Saint Peter's.
Bitter struggle between the emperor and Alexander III and subsequent alliance of both against the Roman people. Occupation of the city and suppression of the power of the Commune by Frederick Barbarossa. A decade of struggle among emperor, pope and citizens, with the appointment of a number of antipopes by the imperial faction. Triumphal return of Alexander III to Rome in 1178.

1188
Compromise on the government of the city between the Commune of Rome and the pope, Clement III, who recognized the autonomy of the Commune.

Under Innocent III, a period of relative calm ensued between Commune and papacy. Appointment of the senator by the pope; however, the city preserved its autonomy and the rights to declare war, conclude treaties, tax the neighboring towns. In 1200, transformation of the Patrimony of Saint Peter into Papal State. In 1215, the fourth Lateran Council – height of the medieval papacy – took place, and a new building development was promoted.
Institution of the hospitals of Santo Spirito in Sassia and San Tommaso in Formis on the Celio and completion of the papal palace.

1220
Coronation of Frederick II as emperor (1220-1250) by Honorius III in Saint Peter's.
In 1216, the institution of the hospital of San Giovanni. Settlement in the city of the Dominican, Franciscans and Cistercians. Transformation of the Savelli house on the Aventine into a fortress by Honorius III Savelli.
After 1230, claims by the Romans on the papacy had by then weakened by the struggles against Frederick II. Works of maintenance in the city by Gregorius IX.

1252-1258
Appointment as senator of a foreigner, Brancaleone degli Andalò, from Bologna, who promoted anti-baronial measures.
In 1254, the institution of the office of Capitano del Popolo (Captain of the People). Beginning of the construction of Santa Maria in Aracoeli and, in 1257, of the new Palazzo Senatorio.

1254-1261	pope Alexander IV Orlando dei Conti di Segni, from Anagni	
1261-1264	pope Urban IV Jacques Pantaléon, from Troyes	
1265-1268	pope Clement IV Guy Foulques Le Gros, from Saint-Gilles-sur-Rhône	1265-1284
1271-1276	pope Gregorius X Teobaldo Visconti, from Piacenza	Appointment as Senator of Charles of Anjou, a Frenchman, opponent and successor of the
1276	pope Innocent V Pietro di Tarantasia (Savoy)	Hohenstaufen, by the pope.
1276	pope Adrian V Ottobono Fieschi dei Conti di Lavagna, from Genoa	
1276-1277	pope John XXI Pietro di Giuliano (Pietro Ispano), from Lisbon	
1277-1280	pope Nicholas III Giovanni Gaetano Orsini, Roman	
1281-1285	pope Martin IV Simone de Brion, from Montpincé (Brie)	
1285-1287	pope Honorius IV Iacopo Savelli, Roman	
1288-1292	pope Nicholas IV Gerolamo Masci, from Lisciano (Ascoli Piceno)	
1294	pope Celestine V Pietro Angeleri da Morrone, from Isernia	

1294-1303   pope Boniface VIII Benedetto Caetani, from Anagni

1300
Proclamation of the first Jubilee by Boniface VIII.

1303-1304   pope Benedict XI Niccolò Boccalini, from Treviso

1303
Foundation of the *Studium Urbis* (University of Rome). Attack of Anagni and death of the pope in Rome.

AVIGNON PAPACY (1305-1377)

1305-1314   pope Clement V Bertrand de Goth, from Villandraut

1305
Transfer of the papacy and the papal Curia from Rome to Avignon.

1308
Fire in San Giovanni in Laterano.

1312
Harsh contention between Orsini and Colonna for supremacy over the city that ended with the removal of both. Establishment in Rome of a popular and anti-baronial government headed by the Capitano del Popolo Jacopo Stefaneschi. Imperial coronation of Henry VII and struggles in the city between guelphs (with the pope) and ghibellines (with the emperor).

1316-1334   pope John XXII Jacques Arnaud d'Euse, from Cahors

1328
The Capitano del Popolo, Sciarra Colonna, and the antipope, Nicholas V, crowned as emperor Ludwig of Bavaria in Saint Peter's.

1339
Foundation of the hospital of San Giacomo in Augusta.

1334-1342   pope Benedict XII Jacques Fournier, from Saverdun

1341
Coronation of Petrarch as poet in the Capitol.

1347
Cola di Rienzo took power and was given full authority and the title of Tribune that he would keep only for a very short time (from May 20 to December 15), promoting anti-baronial measures.

1342-1352 pope Clement VI
Pierre Roger de Rosières, from Château Maumont

1348-1349

Plague in Rome and construction of the steps of Santa Maria in Aracoeli as a votive offering by the Roman people. Earthquake in the city with the destruction of part of the Colosseum and of the top of the tower of the Conti.

		1350 Celebration of the second Jubilee with the pope absent from Rome.
1352-1362	pope Innocent VI Etienne d'Aubert, from Mont	
		1353-1354 Uprising of the Roman people against the barons. In 1354, Cola di Rienzo returned and met with a violent death.
		1355 Coronation of Charles IV of Bohemia as emperor.
		1358 Stability of the popular regime with the institution of the *Sette Riformatori* (Seven Reformers) and the government of the *Felice Società dei Balestrieri e Pavesati*, in office until 1398.
1362-1370	pope Urban V Guillaume de Grimoard, from Château de Grisac	**1360** Promulgation of the first statutes of Rome.
		1361 New fire in San Giovanni in Laterano.
		1367-1370 The papacy (Urban V) returned, although not definitively, to Rome. The curia, however, remained in Avignon where Gregorius XI would later reside.
1370-1378	pope Gregorius XI Pierre Roger de Beaufort, from Château Maumont	
1378-1389	pope Urban VI Bartolomeo Prignano, from Naples	**1378** Election in April of an Italian pontiff (Urban VI), under the pressure of the Romans. However, election at the same time (in August) of another pope, the French Clement VII (1378-1394, Roberto dei Conti, from Genevois). Beginning of the Great Schism, that would end in 1417 with pope Martin V (1417-1431).
1389-1404	pope Boniface IX Pietro Tomacelli, from Naples	Calling of a Jubilee in 1390 by the pope. Arrest and execution of the leaders of a popular revolt against Boniface IX that put en end to the autonomy of the Commune, that was reduced to an exclusively administrative organ.

—Paola Rossi